CONTENTS

Page   CD Track

Introduction 1
   About this Book 1
   About the CD 1
   Icon Legend 3

Section 1 • Preparation **4**
   Chapter 1: Anatomy of the Drumset 4
     Drums 5
       Bass Drum 5
       Snare Drum 5
       Tom-toms 5
     Cymbals 6
       Ride Cymbal 6
       Crash Cymbal 6
       Hi-hat Cymbals 7
       Special Effects Cymbals 7
     Hardware 7
       Bass Drum Pedal 7
       Hi-hat Pedal 7
       Snare Drum Stands 7
       Cymbal Stands 9
       Tom Holders 9
       Rack Systems 10
       Thrones 10
     Putting It All Together 10

   Chapter 2: Drumsticks 13
     Wood and Synthetic Sticks 13
     Beads 14
     Selecting Sticks 14

   Chapter 3: Practicing 16
     Practice Tools 17
       Practice Pads 17
       Metronome 17
       Recorder 17
     Warming Up 18

Section 2 • Playing, Part 1 . . . .**19**
   Chapter 4: Holding the Sticks 19
     Matched Grip 19
     Traditional Grip 20
     Making the Stroke 21
       Matched Grip – Both Hands 21
       Traditional Grip – Left Hand 21

Chapter 5: Reading Music 22
Why Read Music? 22
Notation 23
Pulse and Meter 24
Note and Rest Values 25
Rests 25
Triplets and Tuplets 25
Dotted Notes 26
Other Time Signatures 27
Quarter Time 27
Eighth Time 27
Cut-time 28
Odd Times 28
Expression Marks 29
Dynamics 29
Accents 30
Crescendos and Diminuendos 30
Other Musical Symbols 30
Repeats 30
First and Second Endings 31
Slashes 31
D.S., D.C., Sign, Fine, and Coda 32

Chapter 6: Playing with the Hands and Feet 34
Playing Snare Drum 34
Sticking 34
Alternating 34
Right-hand Lead 34
Which to Use? 34   1–3
Playing Snare Drum with Ride Cymbal or Hi-hat 37
Playing with the Feet 40
Bass Drum 40
Hi-hat 40
Coordinating Bass Drum and Hi-hat 40
Double Bass Drum 41

Chapter 7: Multi-Limb Playing 42
Time and Feel 42   4–8
Combining the Limbs 43
Quarter-note Feel 43   9
Eighth-note Feel 43   10–11
Sixteenth-note Feel 44   12–13
Shuffle Feel 44   14

Section 3 • Playing, Part 2 . . . . **45**

Chapter 8: Moving Around the Drumset .45
Real Estate 45
"Around the Kit" Fills 45   15–16

ALL ABOUT

SPECIAL CD INCLUDES OVER 90 TRACKS FEATURING LOTS OF GREAT SONGS!

DRUMS

MAR 2007

A FUN AND SIMPLE GUIDE TO PLAYING DRUMS

by Rick Mattingly

ISBN-13: 978-1-4234-0818-5
ISBN-10: 1-4234-0818-7

HAL•LEONARD® CORPORATION

7777 W. BLUEMOUND RD. P.O. BOX 13819 MILWAUKEE, WI 53213

Visit Hal Leonard Online at **www.halleonard.com**

FUNNY STUFF

1) Q: What do you call someone who hangs out with musicians?
   A: A drummer.

2) Q: How many drummers does it take to change a light bulb?
   A: None. They have machines that can do that now.

3) A drummer walks into a library and says, "Give me a burger, fries, and a large cola." The librarian responds, "Sshhhh. Don't you know where you are? This is a library!" The drummer, very embarrassed, says in a whisper, "Sorry. Give me a burger, fries, and a large cola."

4) A trombone player wanted to torture the drummer behind him, so he hid one of the drummer's sticks. After looking around for a few minutes in panic, the drummer fell to his knees, raised his eyes to heaven, held up his remaining stick, and said, "Thank you, Lord, for making me a conductor!"

5) Inside the stockade, the soldiers are startled to hear tribal war drums. "I don't like the sound of those drums," the sergeant tells the corporal. But a voice comes out of the forest and says, "Give us a break, he's not our regular drummer."

6) Two girls are walking down the road when they hear, "Psst! Down here!" They look down and see a frog, who says, "If you kiss me I'll turn into a famous drummer and make you rich and famous!" One of the girls reaches down, grabs the frog, and stuffs it in her purse. The other girl says, "Aren't you going to kiss him?" The first girl says, "No way! A talking frog is worth more than a famous drummer any day."

7) Q: What's the difference between a drum machine and a drummer?
   A: You only have to punch the information into the drum machine once!

8) Q: Why is a drum machine better than a drummer?
   A: Because it keeps a steady beat and won't try to steal your girlfriend.

9) A man goes to Africa for a vacation. As he gets off the plane, he hears drumming in the background. He asks someone, "What's the deal with the drums?" but the person just says, "Very bad if drums stop." No matter where the man goes, he hears the drums, but whenever he asks about it, the answer is always the same: "Very bad if drums stop." Then, one day, the drums suddenly cease. Everyone looks alarmed. "What's going to happen now?" the man asks. "Very bad," is the reply. "Now comes bass solo."

10) Q: What's the most common thing a drummer says when he's working?
    A: "Would you like fries with that?"

11) Johnny to his mom: "I want to be a drummer when I grow up."
    Mom to Johnny: "You can't do both."

12) Q: Why was the drummer so proud when he finished his jigsaw puzzle in six months?
    A: The box said "3 to 5 years."

13) Q: What's the difference between a drummer and government bonds?
    A: Government bonds eventually mature and earn money.

14) Q: What's the definition of a gentleman?
    A: Someone who knows how to play the drums—but doesn't.

15) Q: What's the difference between a large pizza and a drummer?
    A: The pizza can feed a family of four.

Chapter 9: Fills and Solos 49
   Fills 49   17–18
   Solos 52
      "The End" (The Beatles) 52
      "Take Five" (Dave Brubeck Quartet) 53

Chapter 10: Swing 54
   Swing Notation 54
   Feel and Expression 55

Chapter 11: More than Drumsticks 56
   Brushes 56   19–20
   Mallets 58
   Alternate Sticks 58

Chapter 12: Advanced Playing 59
   Drums Are Easy?! 59
   Two-bar and Four-bar Phrases 59
   Playing the Form 60
   Developing the Groove 61
   Ghost Notes 61   21
   Mixed Meters 61   22–23
   Phrasing over the Barline 62
   Polyrhythms 63   24–25
   Pushing and Pulling 64

Chapter 13: Double-Kick Technique and Beats 65
   Double Pedal vs. Two Bass Drums 65
   Lead with the Left or Lead with the Right? 65
   Notation 65
   Patterns and Grooves 66   26–29

Chapter 14: Latin and World Percussion 67
   Timbales 67
   Cowbell 67
   Agogos 67
   Bongos 68
   Woodblock 68
   Pedal-operated Instruments 68
   Shakers and Maracas 68
   Tambourines 68   30

Section 4 • Styles **69**

Chapter 15: Early Rock 'n' Roll 69
   Shuffle Beats 69   31–32
   Straight Beats 69
      "Oh, Pretty Woman" (Roy Orbison) 70
      "Come Together" (The Beatles) 70
      "Please Please Me" (The Beatles) .70
   The Bo Diddley Beat 71   33–34

Chapter 16: Blues 72
   Blues Shuffle 72   35–39
      "The Thrill Is Gone" (B.B. King) 74
      "Third Degree" (Eric Clapton) 74
      "Blues Leave Me Alone" (Eric Clapton) 74

Chapter 17: Jazz 75
   Swing Ride 75   40–43
   The Role of the Bass Drum 76
   Independence 77   44–45
   Time, Feel, and Rhythm 79
      Anticipated Beats 79   46
      Breaking Up the Time 80   47
      Two Feel and Four Feel 80
      Double-time and Half-time Feels 81   48–49
   Other Time Signatures 81
      Jazz Waltz 81   50
      Odd Time 82   51–52
   Soloing and Trading Fours 83
   Fusion 83   53

Chapter 18: Latin 85
   Afro-Cuban 85
      Cha-Cha-Cha 86   54
      Rumba 86   55
      Mambo 86
      New York Mozambique 86
      Songo 86   56
      Nanigo 86   57
      Mozambique 87   58
      Salsa 87
   Brazilian 87
      Samba 87   59–60
      Bossa Nova 88   61
      Baiao 88
      Partido Alto 88
      Batucada 88   62
   Other Latin Rhythms 89
      Beguine 89   63
      Tango 89   64
      Bolero 89   65
      Reggae 89   66
        "Don't Stand So Close to Me" (The Police) 90
        "Roxanne" (The Police) 90

Chapter 19: Rock 91
   Quarter-note Ride 91   67–71
      "Born to Be My Baby" (Bon Jovi) 91
      "Zero" (Smashing Pumpkins) 92
      "Mississippi Queen" (Mountain) 93

"Detroit Rock City" (Kiss) 93
"Smells Like Teen Spirit" (Nirvana) 94
Eighth-note Ride 94   72
"Message in a Bottle" (Police) 95
"Hurts So Good" (John Cougar Mellencamp) 95
"Sweet Child o' Mine" (Guns N' Roses) 96
"Back Home" (Booker T. & The MG's) 96
"Jump" (Van Halen) 96
"Shattered" (Rolling Stones) 96
"Authority Song" (John Cougar Mellencamp) 97
"Pour Some Sugar On Me" (Def Leppard) .97
"She's on Fire" (Train) 97
"Barracuda" (Heart) 97
Sixteenth-note Ride 97   73
"Swingtown" (Steve Miller Band) 99
"The Zephyr Song" (Red Hot Chili Peppers) 99
"Minor Thing" (Red Hot Chili Peppers) 99

Chapter 20: Progressive Rock 100
Well-Known Drummers 100
Progressive Rock-styled Drum Beats 100   74–79
"Times Like These" (Foo Fighters) 101
"Silent Talking" (Yes) 101
"Song for America" (Kansas) 102
"Watcher of the Skies" (Genesis) 102
"In the Dead of Night" (UK) 102
"Frame by Frame" (King Crimson) 103

Chapter 21: Funk 104
Delayed Backbeats 104   80–81
"Cold Sweat, Pt. 1" (James Brown) 105
Sixteenth-note Grooves 105   82
"Soul Vaccination" (Tower of Power) 106
Linear Beats 106   83–86
"Peg" (Steely Dan) 107
"Funny Vibe" (Living Colour) 107
"Soul Power" (James Brown) 107

Section 5 • Far-Out Stuff **108**

Chapter 22: Special Effect Cymbals and Drums 108
Special Effect Cymbals 108
Splash 108
China 108
Sizzle 108
Swish 109
Flatride 109
Stacked Cymbals: Mounting Two Cymbals Together 109   87
Additional Drums 110
Auxiliary Snare Drums 110

Toms 110
Timbales 110
Electronic Pads 111
Additional Percussion 111

Chapter 23: Extended Techniques and Special Effects 112
Rimshot Variations 112
Cross-stick 112
Stick-shot 112
Rim Click 112
Drum Rolls 112   88–90
Ghost Notes 113
Hi-hat Splash 114
Playing with the Hands 114
Bowing Cymbals 115
Changing Drum Pitches 115
Junk 115
Playing Outside the Time 116

Chapter 24: Drum Rudiments 117
Roll Rudiments 117
Diddle Rudiments 118
Flam Rudiments 118
Drag Rudiments 118
"50 Ways to Leave Your Lover" (Paul Simon) 119
"Lowdown in the Street" (ZZ Top) 119

Section 6 • Song Transcriptions **121**
"Walk This Way" (Aerosmith) 121   91
"No Reply at All" (Genesis) 125   92
"Smoke on the Water" (Deep Purple) 134   93
"Cissy Strut" (The Meters) 139   94
"Nice to Know You" (Incubus) 141   95

Section 7 • The Gig **147**

Chapter 25: Performance Etiquette 147
What to Wear 147
What to Bring 147
Show Up on Time 147
Stay in Your Place 148
Be Dependable 148
Recommendations 149

Chapter 26: On the Job 150
Warming Up 150
Showmanship 150
Faking It 151
Equipment Failures 152
Broken Sticks 152
Broken Heads 152

Pedal Problems 153
Backups 153
Preventive Maintenance 153
Back-up Essentials 154

Chapter 27: Opportunities 155
Versatility 155
Drumming and Singing 155
Finding a Gig 156
Recording 156
Getting Replaced 157

Section 8 • Equipment **158**

Chapter 28: History of the Drumset 158
Origins 158
Early Drumsets 158
Early Jazz Drumkits .159
R&B and Rock 'n' Roll Kits 159
Electronic Kits 160
Modern Drumsets 160

Chapter 29: Types and Sizes of Drumsets 161
Jazz 161
Classic Rock and Country 161
Hard Rock, Metal, and Fusion 162
Progressive Rock 162

Chapter 30: Brands and Models 163
Make and Model "Levels" 163
Drum Shell Types 164
Leading Drumset Manufacturers 164
Cymbal Makers 166

Chapter 31: Thrones 170
Comfort and Function 170
Seat Shapes 170
Throne Height 170
Back Support 171

Section 9 • Care and Maintenance **172**

Chapter 32: Drumheads and Tuning 172
Drumhead Types 172
Single-ply Heads .172
Double-ply Heads 172
Specialty Heads 173
Tuning 173
Tuning Toms 174
Tuning the Snare Drum 175
Tuning the Bass Drum 175
Acoustics 176

Chapter 33: Repairs 177
   Stripped Lugs, Screws, and Wingnuts 177
   Cracked Cymbals 178
   Cracked Drumshell 178
   Broken Drumheads 178
   Noisy Lugs 179
   General Maintenance 179
   Cleaning Cymbals and Drums 179

Chapter 34: Cases 181
   Bags 181
   Fiber Cases 182
   Molded Cases 182
   Road Cases 182
   Moving Aids 182

Section 10 • Who's Who **184**
   Gene Krupa 184
   Buddy Rich 185
   Max Roach 185
   Elvin Jones 186
   Tony Williams 186
   Ringo Starr 187
   Hal Blaine 187
   Billy Cobham 187
   Ginger Baker 188
   John Bonham 188
   Steve Gadd 189
   Neil Peart 189

Appendix **190**
   Reference Sheet 190
   Who's Who Big List 192
   Track Listing 197
   About the Author 198

INTRODUCTION

ABOUT THIS BOOK

All About Drums is designed to serve as a handbook for aspiring as well as more established drummers. For those who are new to drumset, the book has plenty of basic information on such topics as how to hold sticks, the different instruments that comprise modern drumsets, which drums and cymbals to use for different styles of music, how to read music, how to play by ear, how to tune drums, practicing, warming up, rudiments, and brief bios of some of the most important drummers in history, including recommended recordings.

For those who are already involved with drumming, the book explores a wide variety of musical styles—including rock, jazz, and Latin music—and also gives practical advice about opportunities for drummers, proper behavior on a gig, maintaining and repairing drums and cymbals, electronic drums, and transporting equipment.

Essentially, *All About Drums* is an owner's manual for drummers that can serve as a valuable reference text throughout a drummer's career, whether he or she drums as a hobby or plays professionally.

The book is arranged in a "progressive" order, so that you can start at the beginning and work your way straight through it. But, especially if you already play, you can certainly skip around and focus on specific chapters when you need particular information.

This is not, quite honestly, the only drum book you will ever need. Each style of music can be studied for years and years, and as you decide on the style or styles you want to explore, you will want to avail yourself of additional books and instructional DVDs that focus on that style or styles. But *All About Drums* will provide a framework you can use to build your own drumming personality, and will give you a solid foundation in a wide variety of drumming-related areas.

There is quite a bit of music in this book, because ultimately that's what playing drums is about. So when you're going through these pages, have a pair of sticks handy and don't be too far away from a drumset or practice pad. The most important goal of *All About Drums* is to get you playing!

ABOUT THE CD

All About Drums includes a 95-track CD containing demonstrations of selected exercises and grooves from the book, along with five complete play-along songs. The music that was picked for the CD tracks was chosen to be representative of the different styles that the book explores. So although a particular example might not be demonstrated, there will be an example that is close enough that you should be able to figure out the variations that are used in related examples.

The CD tracks will also help you learn to read music, because every CD track (including the five complete songs) is notated in the book. Some of the CD examples are very easy and you can probably learn to play them just by listening, but look at the music on those easy ones to see how drum notation works; then you will have an easier time figuring out the more complex examples.

In addition to the examples that are demonstrated on the CD, the book also contains notated examples of the drum beats from a wide variety of well-known popular songs. So whenever possible, get a copy of the original recording of the song to hear how the drummer made it sound and made it feel.

It is often said that the best musicians are the best listeners, so spend a lot of time listening to the CD that comes with this book, recordings of other songs notated in the book, and anything else you can find that has great drumming. Doing that will help you become a great drummer as well.

Credits

Section 6, "Song Transcriptions" recorded by Jake Johnson:
   Drums by Scott Schroedl
   Guitars by Doug Boduch
   Bass by Tom McGirr
   Keyboards by Warren Wiegratz

All other tracks performed by Rick Mattingly, Jeff McAllister, and Jason Tieman.

ICON LEGEND

Included in every *All About* book are several icons to help you on your way. Keep an eye out for these.

AUDIO
This icon signals you to a track on the accompanying CD.

TRY THIS
Included with this icon are various bits of helpful advice about playing the drums.

EXTRAS
This includes additional information on various topics that may be interesting and useful, but not necessarily essential.

DANGER!
Here, you'll learn how to avoid injury and keep your equipment from going on the fritz.

ORIGINS
Interesting little historical blurbs are included for fun and background information.

NUTS & BOLTS
Included with this last icon are tidbits on the fundamentals or building blocks of music.

Preparation

CHAPTER 1
ANATOMY OF THE DRUMSET

What's Ahead:
- Drums
- Cymbals
- Hardware
- Putting it all together

Drumsets are cool! They are usually the focal point of a stage setup—and not just because they're in the middle and take up the most space. Drumsets are fascinating to behold.

Front and center is the bass drum, its large front head aimed out at the crowd, delivering the punch and pulse that makes people want to get up and dance. Above and around the bass drum are the other drums, some sitting flat, some tilted, with shiny lugs and rims reflecting the lights as they emit the backbeats, fills, and solos that make the music come alive.

Angled up above are the bronze-colored cymbals, which produce the loudest, most vibrant explosions as well as the softest, most delicate colors. The crate-like amplifier cabinets don't stand a chance of being noticed next to the wonder of a drumset.

And for all their posing and running around the stage, singers and guitarists can't match the visual excitement that drummers provide, with arms and sticks flying in every direction, and yet perfectly choreographed with the music. Drummers project power and authority, and it's no wonder that drummers are said to be in the "driver's seat."

Unlike, say, guitars, which despite their many shapes, sizes, and colors, all have about the same number of available notes and the same standard tuning, drumsets can range from very small, with a minimum of drums and cymbals, to extremely large. In fact, you've probably already noticed that each drummer has a slightly different setup.

Nevertheless, there are a few basics that are common to just about every drumset. In most situations, a drummer needs at least one bass drum, one snare drum, two tom-toms, a ride cymbal, a crash cymbal, and a hi-hat.

Before we take a quick look at each basic element of the drumset, we need to learn some "drum lingo." When drummers talk about a kit in terms of how many "pieces" it has, they are only talking about the drums. Cymbals and any other sound effects are not included in the count. So when you see an ad for a "five-piece drumset," unless the ad specifically says "includes cymbals," the price only covers the drums included in a typical five-piece kit: a bass drum, a snare drum, two rack toms, and one floor tom. The cymbals are going to cost you extra. And it probably won't come with a throne (the stool the drummer sits on), either. So be prepared when you go shopping for your first kit.

The elements of a standard drumset are usually divided into three categories: drums, cymbals, and hardware. Let's look at each.

DRUMS

Bass Drum

The bass drum is the foundation of the kit, and it is the biggest member of the drumset. That's the drum that sits on its side at the front of the kit. (Some drummers like to use the front head as a billboard to display the name or logo of the band—or their own name!) The bass drum is played with a foot pedal that is usually operated by the player's right foot. Because it is played with the foot, some people call the bass drum the "kick drum."

Many hard rock drummers use two bass drums for added power. You can also play double bass drum patterns on a single bass drum by means of a double bass drum pedal (more about that in Chapter 6).

> Although most people associate double bass drums with hard rock styles, the first person to popularize the use of two bass drums was big-band jazz drummer Louie Bellson.

The most popular bass drum for rock has 22-inch diameter heads and either a 14-inch or 16-inch shell depth. If you are playing jazz or acoustic music, you might want a bass drum with 20-inch or even 18-inch heads. For extra power in heavily amplified settings, and for tremendous bottom end, go with a bass drum that has 24-inch heads. Bigger and smaller drums are available, but really small and REALLY LARGE bass drums are generally only used for special effects or in very specific situations.

Snare Drum

The snare drum provides the loud "crack" sound that, combined with the bass drum notes, defines the basic beat of a song. The snare drum is placed between your legs so that it is directly in front of you. Most snare drums are 14 inches in diameter with shells that are from 5 inches to 6 1/2 inches deep, but other sizes are available. Many snare drums have metal shells for a brighter, more cutting sound, but some drummers prefer wood-shell snare drums for their added body and warmth of tone. A snare drum has several strands of wire, cable, nylon, or gut—called "snares"—stretched across its bottom head, which give the drum its distinctive "sizzling" sound.

Tom-toms

Most drumsets have several tom-toms (or simply "toms"), which are tuned to different pitches. Toms are most often used for fills and solos, but can also be used along with the bass drum and snare drum to define the basic beat.

Tom-toms are often divided into two categories: *Rack toms* (sometimes called *mounted toms*) are generally smaller drums that are mounted on the bass drum or suspended from some type of rack or holder. *Floor toms* are generally larger and deeper drums that have their own legs and sit on (guess what?) the floor.

Small drumsets used for jazz often have just two toms: a rack tom and a floor tom. Most standard drumkits have three toms: two rack toms and a floor tom. From there, you can add on as many toms as you can afford—or reach!

Snare Drum or Drumset?

It used to be standard practice for drum teachers to make students start out on just a snare drum. Then, after a year (or more), they were "allowed" to start learning drumset. To me, that's like telling someone who wants to learn to play basketball that he should just dribble a ball for a few months to see if he likes it, and then maybe he can get a hoop.

I have started many students over the years, and average students are generally able to play a simple timekeeping pattern using both hands (on ride cymbal and snare drum) and at least one foot (on bass drum) by the second lesson.

There are situations in which I do, in fact, start students out on just a snare drum. These are students who do not have a drumset, but who want to join their school band. In that situation, they will be playing snare drum by itself, so it makes perfect sense for them to start out just on snare drum.

But at some point, most of those students acquire a drumset. As much as they know already about playing snare drum, it generally takes those students just as long to learn that first drumset beat as it does an absolute beginner who has never played at all.

Yes, snare drum is one of the most important parts of the drumset. And yes, developing good snare drum technique will make you a better overall set player. But good drumset playing is also about coordination of all four limbs and about timekeeping. You need a full drumset to develop those abilities properly.

CYMBALS

Ride Cymbal

Ride cymbals often provide a "cushion" for the music. A good ride cymbal will do two things: have enough *definition* (clarity of sound) that the rhythm pattern played on it is distinct, and have enough *overtones* (higher pitches above the main pitch which help give the sound its character) to help fill out the sound of the band (without losing the definition in a "wash").

Ride cymbals most typically range in diameter from 18 to 22 inches. The most popular ride cymbals by far are 20-inch, medium-weight rides. They usually have a good balance of overtones and definition.

Most rock drummers only use one ride cymbal, because they often ride on the hi-hat. Jazz drummers will often have two or even three ride cymbals, because they seldom ride on the hi-hat, and while rock drummers generally propel the music with the snare drum and bass drum, jazz drummers propel the music primarily with the ride cymbal. Therefore, jazz drummers like to be able to change the sound by using more than one ride.

Crash Cymbal

Crash cymbals provide the explosive punctuation marks in music. Most drummers have at least two or three crashes for different effects. Crashes generally range from about 14 inches in diameter to 19 inches, with 16- and 18-inch crashes being the most popular.

Some drummers go for heavy crash cymbals in the hopes that they won't break as easily. But heavy crash cymbals often sound "gongy," and they don't respond very quickly. Thin crash cymbals have the fastest response, but their sound is often, well…thin. Most drummers go with medium-thin or medium crash cymbals, which have a good balance between fast response and fullness of tone, and will stand up to reasonably hard hitting.

Crash cymbals tend to get broken the most because of the power with which they are struck. But there are a couple of things you can do to prolong the life of your crash cymbal. First, do not clamp your crash cymbal down too tightly. It should be very loose on the stand so that, when you strike it, it has plenty of room to vibrate. Second, do not strike the cymbal with a straight-down motion. Hit it with a sideways, glancing blow. As with drums, you want to strike the cymbal in such a way as to make it vibrate; you don't simply want to have a collision with it!

You might find a cymbal marked "Crash-Ride," indicating that it can be used as either a crash cymbal or a ride cymbal. But the qualities that make a good ride cymbal are different from the qualities that make a good crash cymbal. So in most cases, a "Crash-Ride" is a mediocre crash and a mediocre ride. If you can't afford a good ride and a good crash right away, decide which one you need the most, buy a good one, and save money to buy the other one later. If you are playing a lot of pop music or jazz, you'll want to start with a good ride cymbal. But if you are playing a lot of heavy rock, you can do most of your riding on the hi-hat, and so you might want to get a good crash before you invest in a good ride.

Cymbals don't always sound the same close up as they do from a distance. So when picking out a new cymbal at a music store, narrow your choices down to two or three. Then have a friend or the salesperson play them while you stand at a distance and listen. You might even want to do this with your back to the cymbals so that you make your choice entirely by sound.

Hi-hat Cymbals

The hi-hat is made up of two cymbals and a pedal. (We'll talk about the pedal under the "Hardware" section, which follows.) The most popular size for hi-hat cymbals is 14 inches, with 13-inch hi-hats being the next most popular choice. There are a variety of hi-hat cymbal models, but most have a heavier bottom cymbal and a lighter-weight top cymbal. Having a heavier bottom cymbal helps you get a good "chick" sound when you bring the cymbals together with the pedal. Having a lighter top cymbal (often a medium) helps you get more overtones when striking the hi-hat with a stick, thus producing a "fatter" sound.

Special Effects Cymbals

In addition to ride, crash, and hi-hat cymbals, many drummers will include one or more "special effects" cymbals in their setups, such as China cymbals, sizzle cymbals, and splash cymbals. For more information on these, see Chapter 22.

HARDWARE

The term "hardware" is generally used in reference to the parts of a drum kit made of metal—but not including cymbals. Hardware includes the stands, holders, and pedals that are used with the kit, and can also refer to thrones, rims, and lugs.

Bass Drum Pedal

By pressing down on a bass drum pedal with your foot, a *beater* strikes the drum, producing a loud "thud" or "boom" (depending on how you have the drum tuned and muffled). When it is "at rest," the beater is held away from the head by a spring, and the spring also helps the beater rebound from the head after you make the stroke. The best bass drum pedals have springs that are adjustable so you can get the resistance you want for different playing styles.

Originally, the pedal's footplate was attached to the beater by a leather strap. Back in the late 1960s, a drum technician named Frank Duffy who worked at Ippolito's Drum Shop in New York City experimented with replacing the leather strap with a piece of bicycle chain and using a small bicycle gear to help move the beater. This became known as the "chain-drive" pedal, and it is offered by several manufacturers today. Many drummers feel that chain-drive pedals are faster than pedals with leather straps. Some chain-drive pedals have two chains mounted side-by-side to help prevent breakage.

During the 1970s, the double bass drum pedal was invented, which allowed drummers to play double bass patterns on a single bass drum. The left pedal, known as the "remote," is generally placed next to the hi-hat pedal, but its beater is right next to the main beater.

Remote pedals are also available that allow drummers such as Alex Van Halen and Terry Bozzio to have additional bass drums mounted off to the sides of their setups.

Hi-hat Pedal

In addition to serving as a stand for the two hi-hat cymbals, the hi-hat pedal allows you to play the hi-hat with your foot (usually the left foot), bringing the two cymbals together to provide a "chick" sound. You also use the foot pedal to hold the cymbals together while you ride on the hi-hat. By holding the cymbals together tightly, you can get a well-defined "click"-type ride sound, or you can hold the cymbals in a looser position to get what drummers call a "sloshy" sound (like the sound John Bonham got in Led Zeppelin's song "Rock and Roll"). You can also get a "bark" by opening the hi-hat with your foot as the top cymbal is being struck by a stick and then quickly closing the cymbals with the pedal.

To aid drummers with large setups who need to have their hi-hat pedal in a comfortable position, but prefer (or need) to have the hi-hat cymbals mounted a little farther away than usual, some companies offer remote hi-hats. Instead of the pedal and cymbals being connected by a straight metal rod, the pedal assembly is separate and connected to the cymbal-mounting assembly by a flexible cable. Some drummers use these so that the pedal can be operated with the left foot even though the cymbals are mounted on the right side of the kit.

There are also units without pedals that allow you to mount a pair of hi-hat cymbals in a closed position anywhere on the kit. Some drummers use these in addition to a regular pedal-operated hi-hat for an alternate closed hi-hat sound.

Snare Drum Stands

Snare drum stands usually have a "basket" that grips the bottom snare drum rim in three places. The basket may be tilted so that you can angle the drum toward you (which can help avoid accidental rimshots), away from you (which can help if you almost always play rimshots), or downward to the right, if you use traditional grip. (Of course, you can also adjust the basket so the drum is perfectly flat, which is probably how the majority of drummers do it.)

The legs of the stand need to spread wide enough to give the drum stability (remember, you will be really slamming this drum at times), but you don't want the legs to extend out so far that they interfere with your placement of the bass drum and hi-hat pedals. Some stands have "flat base" designs, meaning that they have three legs that extend out and sit flat on the floor. Others have tripod designs. For maximum strength and stability, go for double-braced legs. But if you don't play very hard, double-braced legs might be unnecessary. They weigh more and take up more room in your trap case, so consider how portable you need to be and don't buy bigger and heavier stands than you need.

Cymbal Stands

Cymbal stands come in two basic styles: straight stands and boom stands. *Straight stands* look like their names: they go straight up, and usually have three sections that telescope into each other for packing, which allow for a wide range of heights.

Boom stands are designed for large setups in which you want to hang a cymbal over your drums, but don't have the floor room to get a straight stand close enough to your kit to do so. A boom stand usually has two or three "straight" sections, and it also has an "arm" that extends at an angle in relation to the main stand. You mount your cymbal on one end of the arm, and the other end usually has a counterweight to help balance the stand so that the weight of the cymbal doesn't make it tip over.

At the top of every cymbal stand (and on one end of a boom arm) is a cymbal tilter, which allows you to angle your cymbal if you wish. Most drummers angle their cymbals at least a little bit, but you don't want to angle them too much or you will be striking them at an awkward angle that could lead to breakage.

Always make sure that the *cymbal post* (the top of the tilter that goes through the hole in the cymbal) has a rubber or plastic sleeve around it. That helps protect the cymbal from metal-to-metal contact with the stand. Underneath the cymbal there should be a felt washer, also to protect the cymbal.

Cymbal tilters generally have a wing nut at the top, but don't tighten it down very much. Cymbals should be free to vibrate so that their sound isn't choked and they don't crack from taking a bad hit.

Tom Holders

Rack toms have various types of mounts on their sides so that they can be attached to various types of stands or holders. Older drums often had mounts screwed onto their shells. Some of them slid onto clips or posts, while others attached to arms that extended into the drum shell.

In recent years, more drums have featured "suspension" mounts, pioneered by the RIMS mounts of the 1980s. These mounts are attached to the drum's rim, rather than its shell, and nothing penetrates the shell. This allows the shell to have maximum resonance.

Often, one or two rack toms will be mounted on top of the bass drum via a holder that extends into the bass drum shell. Since most modern bass drums are muffled to produce a "thud" rather than a "boom," any loss of resonance this produces in the bass drum is minimized. But some drummers prefer to leave their bass drums free of mounting hardware, so they mount their rack toms on floor stands or on rack systems.

Traditionally, floor toms had three brackets mounted on the shell, each of which held a leg. Today, some "floor" toms are suspended from stands or rack systems.

Rack Systems

Rack systems generally consist of one or more beams from which a drummer can mount a variety of toms, cymbals, and other devices (such as cowbells and woodblocks). One advantage of a rack system is that if you have a large setup, you won't have the legs of multiple floor stands getting in each other's way. Rack systems also allow you to keep the bass drum "free," so that if you suddenly need to change a head, you can just pull the drum out from under the rack without having to dismount any toms or cymbals.

Thrones

I've known drummers who have spent thousands of dollars on the finest drums and cymbals money can buy, then purchased the cheapest throne they could find. Don't do that! Get a sturdy, comfortable throne. You are going to be spending a lot of time sitting on it, and you don't want it falling over or causing pain in your backside.

Make sure the legs are sturdy (double-braced legs are a good idea), and that they have enough spread to support you. Remember, you are going to be moving a lot when you play, and you need solid support.

The seat should be comfortable, but not so soft that you sink down into it. A too-soft cushion will not give you the support you need. Seats come in various shapes, the most popular being round, followed by saddle-shaped (like a bicycle seat). Choose the one that feels best to you and that allows total freedom of movement for your legs. Seats also come in different sizes. Choose one according to the size of, er…the part of you that's going to be sitting on it.

Some thrones are available with back rests. You don't want to be leaning back when you play, but in between songs it can be nice to settle back for a minute or two and rest your lower back.

PUTTING IT ALL TOGETHER

When first setting up your drumset, arrange the various drums, cymbals, pedals, and throne to fit your body. Don't make your body fit the setup!

Start with your throne. It should be high enough that your thighs are angled downward slightly. This will give you the most control of the pedals. Do NOT sit so low that your knees are pointing up. You will lose a lot of power and also suffer fatigue. By the same token, don't have your throne so high that you are "tiptoeing" on the pedals.

Should a "Lefty" Set Up in Reverse?

Sometimes you see left-handed players who have everything on their kits reversed. But a lot of left-handed drummers set up just like right-handed drummers. The biggest advantage is that if you play the standard setup, you will be comfortable behind most drumkits. The fact is, you won't always be able to play your own kit!

Sometimes, when there is more than one band on a show, and the stage isn't very large, bands will share drumsets and amplifiers to save space and save time when changing from one band to the next. Also, during auditions, everyone might be asked to play the same kit in the interest of efficiency.

Recording studios sometimes have their own drumkits that are already miked up. If you have to switch everything around just to record a 30-second jingle, then the engineer will have to move all the mics around, too. Time is money in the studio, and if someone decides you're wasting their time, you won't get called back.

If you are invited to "sit in" with a band, you will be expected to jump behind the kit that is on stage, play a song or two, and then let the band's regular drummer take over again. That drummer is being gracious enough to let you play his kit; don't abuse his generosity by moving everything around.

There is nothing wrong with setting up in reverse if you are left-handed. But there is no physical reason why you need to (have you ever seen a left-handed piano?), and your life might be a easier if you are comfortable playing a standard setup.

Avoid "drummer's slouch." You might think it looks cool to "hunch" over your drumset, and you may very well have seen many drummers sit that way. But bad drumming posture can cause serious lower back problems as you get older. So if you hope to play drums for many years to come, sit up straight! Your body will have more freedom of movement, and you won't damage your back muscles and spine.

Once you have your throne at the proper height, place your bass drum and hi-hat so that you can play the pedals comfortably with your feet. (If you have two bass drums or a double bass pedal, make sure you can operate both bass pedals and the hi-hat pedal easily, without having to stretch one of your legs out at an awkward angle.)

Now position the snare drum between your legs. This is the drum you will be playing the most, so you want it in as comfortable as position as possible. Adjust the height so that when you are sitting straight up, your upper arms hang straight down, and your forearms are at a slight downward angle when your sticks are resting on the drum. If the snare drum is too high, you will have to raise your arms to hit it; if it is too low, you will be tempted to slouch.

Adjust your rack toms (or mounted toms) so that you can reach them with a minimum of arm movement. Avoid mounting them too high and then tilting them forward at an extreme angle. That can result in a lot of broken drumheads because your sticks will be striking the tom heads with the points instead of the sides of the beads. Even if you use a round-bead stick, you will be driving the stick into the head if the drum is tilted too much. Just tilt the toms toward you slightly so you can strike the head cleanly without hitting the rim. The toms closest to the snare drum should not be too much higher than the snare so that you don't have to jerk your arms up when doing fast fills that go from snare to toms.

Floor toms are usually positioned at the same height as the snare drum so that it's easy to move straight across when going from snare drum to floor tom. Don't put the floor tom so far to the right that you have to stretch your right arm to reach it. Usually, there is just enough room between your floor tom and snare drum for your right leg to play the bass drum without your thigh or knee rubbing against either the snare drum or floor tom.

You will be playing your hi-hat and ride cymbal as much as your snare drum, so you'll want both of them positioned in such a way so that you do not have to strain to reach them. You should already have the hi-hat placed where your foot can manipulate the pedal easily, but you still have to consider the height of the cymbals. If, like most drummers, you are going to cross your right hand over your left so you can ride on the hi-hat with the right hand while playing snare drum with the left, then you want the hi-hat cymbals high enough to allow plenty of room for your left hand to make the proper motions. If you make your strokes more from your wrist than from your arm (which you should!), you should not have any problems crossing over. But if your arms are having collisions, try raising the hi-hat rather than lowering the snare drum so that you don't end up playing in a "hunched over" position.

The ride cymbal should also be in a position that allows you to play it for long periods without straining your arm muscles. Jazz drummers, who play the ride cymbal a LOT more than they play on the hi-hats, often use just one rack tom so that they can put the ride cymbal where the second rack tom would be. Drummers who have two toms mounted on the bass drum usually put the ride cymbal in between the middle tom and the floor tom. But you have to position it so that it doesn't get in the way when you are doing a fast fill "around the toms." As with the toms, do not position the ride cymbal at an extreme angle because that will interfere with the efficiency of your stroke. You want your stick to "dance" on the ride cymbal, not poke at it. As much as possible, position your ride cymbal so that your upper arm is hanging at a relaxed position when you play it.

Crash cymbals can be positioned higher, but not so high and far away that you have to stretch a lot to reach them. That wears out your muscles and can also interfere with your timing (and what good is a drummer with bad timing?). The best way to strike crash cymbals is with a glancing blow on the edge, so having them up a little higher helps you do that, and avoids bringing the stick straight down on them, which can lead to cracked cymbals!

The more drums and cymbals you have, the more difficult it might be to put everything in an ideal position. So decide which of your instruments you will be playing the most, and put them as close as possible. Instruments that you only use on occasion can be placed a little farther away.

Arrange your drums and cymbals to fit your body. Don't slouch, stretch, or otherwise contort your body to accommodate your setup.

One Instrument

Most drummers have had the experience of people coming up to them and saying, "I don't know how you can play all of those different instruments at the same time!" True, the drumset has a bunch of different drums and cymbals, and yes, each can be considered an instrument in its own right. But when combined, they become a single instrument called the *drumset*.

Look at it this way: A piano has 88 keys, but can you imagine anyone asking pianists how they can play 88 different instruments at the same time? Of course not! The piano is viewed as a single instrument with 88 notes. Likewise, the drumset can be viewed as a single instrument with several different notes.

And what we play with our collection of notes is not all that different than what pianists do. Sometimes we play one note; sometimes we play several notes at the same time, just as a pianist might play a chord. Sometimes we have a rhythmic line going on the ride cymbal while we play another rhythmic line between the bass drum and snare drum, just as a pianist might be playing a melody with the right hand, and a bass line with the left.

Legendary jazz drummer Elvin Jones compared a drumset to the human body in an interview in the book *The Drummer's Time* (Modern Drummer/Hal Leonard): "You can't isolate the different parts of the drumset any more than you can isolate your left leg from the rest of your body," he said. "Your body is one, even though you have two legs, two arms, ten fingers, and all of that. But all of those parts add up to one human being. It's the same with the instrument. People are never going to approach the drumset correctly if they don't start thinking of it as a single musical instrument."

CHAPTER 2
DRUMSTICKS

> ***What's Ahead:***
> - Wood and synthetic sticks
> - Beads
> - Selecting sticks

Drumsticks don't come in all shapes, but they certainly come in a variety of sizes.

The model names on drumsticks can be confusing. You'll see a lot of sticks with names like 5B, 7A, or 2S. At one time (many, many years ago), the A indicated a stick designed for orchestra use, the B designated a stick meant for band use, and an S indicated that the stick was designed for "street" use (i.e., marching band). Therefore, A sticks were a little smaller and lighter, B sticks were a bit beefier, and S sticks resembled miniature baseball bats.

To some extent, those designations are still accurate, but not every manufacturer's 7A (for example) is the same size, and the distinctions between the different models are not as pronounced as they once were. In addition, many sticks are now labeled according to a style of music (rock, jazz, funk), or they have a name meant to convey their "character" (Whackers, Rock Knocker, New Orleans, Groovers, Power House), or they carry the name of the prominent drumset player who uses that model (generally referred to as "signature" models).

So how do you choose your first pair of sticks? With practically every drumstick manufacturer, 5A is the "general" stick. In fact, many drumstick manufacturers and music store owners will tell you that they sell as many 5A's as all the other models combined. So that's a good place to start. After you've been playing a while, you may then decide that you would like to try something lighter, or heavier, or thicker, or thinner, or shorter, or longer, or whatever…but start with a medium-size, general-purpose stick such as a 5A as your reference point.

(danger) Using a stick that is too heavy can cause fatigue, and can even damage your muscles or tendons. A stick that is too thin may cause hand cramps because you have to squeeze more tightly to hold onto it.

WOOD AND SYNTHETIC STICKS

Drumsticks are made from a variety of wood types, with hickory, maple, and oak being the most popular. Many drummers prefer hickory because it has a lot of flex, which helps prevent stick breakage, and absorbs some of the shock of the impact. Maple is a harder wood than hickory, but it is also lighter. Some drummers prefer maple because they like the feel of a fatter stick in their hand, but don't want it to be too heavy. Maple doesn't flex as well as hickory, so maple sticks don't stand up as well to heavy hitting without breaking, and they can transfer more of the shock of the blow into your hands, wrists, and arms. Oak sticks tend to be a little bit heavier than hickory sticks. Oak is also a harder wood than hickory, so it can often stand up to harder playing. But, like maple, it doesn't absorb as much shock as hickory.

Be careful with synthetic sticks that are designed "never to break." Instead of absorbing shock, as wood sticks do, synthetic sticks often transfer the impact shock back into your hands, wrists, and arms, which can cause injury to your body. If you repeatedly drive your stick into a metal drum rim while playing rimshots, it's better to break an inexpensive wood stick than to hurt yourself by having the force of that impact transferred back into your body.

BEADS

Drumsticks have different shaped beads, or tips, that most often fall into one of the following shape categories: acorn, oval, round, or barrel. *Acorn* (also sometimes called *teardrop*) beads are the most versatile: by angling the stick different ways you can get slightly different sounds, especially from ride cymbals. *Round* tips are the most consistent, as they will always produce the same sound no matter what the angle of the stick. They tend to produce a lot of overtones on a ride cymbal, and a fairly large round-bead stick gets a bigger sound from drums. *Oval* and *barrel* tips fall somewhere between acorn and round beads. They are not as versatile as acorn, but not as consistent as round tips. Nevertheless, one of them might fit your playing style and sound preferences perfectly, so you should check them all out.

The difference in tip shape will be most obvious on your ride cymbal, so when shopping for the ultimate stick, you should take your own cymbal to your local drum shop or music store and try out the different sticks on the exact cymbal you will be playing. The stick that makes one cymbal sound the best might not be the perfect stick for a different cymbal.

Some drumsticks have nylon or plastic beads. These produce a brighter, more "pingy" sound on ride cymbals. Nylon tips often rebound a little better than wood tips, and so they are sometimes favored by players who use a lot of double-stroke or buzz rolls. Nylon beads won't wear down or splinter the way wood tips will after long use, though nylon tips sometimes become unglued and fly off.

The *neck* is the portion of the drumstick right below the bead, and it is the thinnest part of the stick. That is where sticks most often break, so if you play hard and loud, make sure you choose a stick with a fairly thick neck.

SELECTING STICKS

When buying sticks, you should roll them on a flat surface, such as a glass counter, to make sure they are not warped. Some manufacturers pre-match their sticks by "pitch pairing" them. This ensures the most consistent sound from a pair of sticks when you are playing on the same surface, such as a snare drum or a practice pad. You can check the pitch of the sticks yourself by tapping the sticks lightly on a countertop or practice pad, and listening for the "ring" of the wood.

Some drummers prefer sticks that are matched by weight. Since they are usually playing cymbal or hi-hat with one stick and snare drum with the other, the pitch doesn't matter as much. If you are extremely concerned about weight, you'll probably need to buy a small scale (such as a postage scale) and take it with you to the music store where you buy your sticks. Generally, however, sticks that are pitch-paired are close enough in weight that you won't notice a difference.

Using Different Drumsticks

Many drummers search for what they consider the perfect stick for their playing style, and once they find it, that's all they ever use. Other drummers have more than one drumstick model in their stickbags. Either approach can be valid.

If you specialize in a single style of music, and all of your playing is with the same band in very similar venues, then always using the same sticks could make a lot of sense. You will certainly feel comfortable with those sticks, and sometimes you can save money by buying them in bulk.

But if you play different styles of music with different bands in different settings, you might want to have an array of stick models. It might be as simple as, for example, using a heavier stick for loud rock gigs and a lighter stick for jazz or pop gigs. Perhaps you prefer wood tips as a rule, but if you are in a setting in which, for whatever reason, your cymbals are not cutting through as well as you would like, switching to a pair of nylon-tip sticks could solve the problem. Even with the same band in the same room, different songs often call for different sounds. Look at all the different sounds your guitar player can get by turning a knob or stomping on a pedal. You can often change the character of your ride cymbal by using sticks with different sizes and shapes of tips.

And don't overlook all the sound colors you can get with various "alternative" striking implements, such as brushes and mallets. (See Chapter 11 for more information on such devices.)

CHAPTER 3
PRACTICING

What's ahead:
- Practice tools
- Warming up

My first teacher used to tell me, "If you want to be a good drummer, don't think about drumming, don't talk about drumming, don't read about drumming, just *put the stick on the drum!*" In other words, *practice*!

We practice to get better, of course. But we can also divide our practice time into categories.

- **Practicing to learn something new.** Too many people spend most of their time playing stuff they can already play and calling that "practice." There's nothing wrong with playing things you know, but the biggest benefit of practicing comes from working on something that you *don't* know.

  When you are trying to learn something new, don't go for marathon practice sessions, because your mind will get tired easily. Instead, practice the new material frequently for short periods of time. For example, working on something new for, say, 15 minutes in the afternoon and another 15 minutes later that evening will do you more good than practicing the same material for 30 minutes straight once a day. Also, be sure you practice every day. Especially with new material, you need to keep reminding your brain and your body how to do it.

- **Practicing to refine something you know a little bit.** Even if there is something we can play pretty well, we can usually play it cleaner, faster, or with a better feel—or maybe we haven't quite got it memorized yet.

- **Practicing for endurance.** This is where you can go back to something you know and see how long you can keep it up. You might even try going through *everything* you know—or at least every song you are going to play at your upcoming gig. Drumming is a very physical activity and a gig can last for three or four hours, so you need a lot of strength and endurance. You also need to learn how to pace yourself, so that you don't blow all of your energy during the first hour.

- **Practicing for fun.** Don't ignore this one! Some people equate "practice" with "work," and if you're enjoying yourself, then it can't be work, and, therefore, it isn't practice. C'mon, we *play* the drums, we don't *work* them. Practicing should be fun, whether you are working on something new that you can't quite handle or just playing along to a record that you love. Yes, practicing can be frustrating when you just can't seem to get something, but relax—just take it slow and you'll get it eventually. Set realistic goals for your practicing so you can feel good about having accomplished something—no matter how small—every time you practice. Real musicians enjoy practicing just as much as they enjoy playing a gig, because they love playing their instrument, no matter what—and getting better is the most fun part of all!

PRACTICE TOOLS

Practice Pads

Many drummers have a practice pad, which enables them to warm up their hands or work on their technique without generating all of the volume that a drum produces. You might want to use a pad because you're a nice person and don't want to bother people who are nearby—especially late at night or early in the morning. Or you might not want people to hear you working out a technique that you can't quite handle yet. Whatever the reason, you should have a pad.

There are several different types of practice pads. A Gladstone pad fits over a drumhead so that the drum is not as loud. It is made of rubber and has a raised section in the middle that has much the same feel as a drumhead. A Gladstone pad can also be laid on a table for quieter practice. Gladstone pads are designed for 14-inch snare drums, but several manufacturers make rubber pads that fit every size of drum in a drumset, and they even have pads for bass drums and cymbals so you can practice on your entire kit whenever you want without bothering your neighbors!

Many practice pads consist of a thin rubber pad that is glued onto a wooden base. These are very portable and are usually the quietest pads. Tunable practice pads consist of an actual drumhead mounted on a plastic or metal frame. They are louder than rubber pads, but they are still much quieter than a drum.

Metronome

A metronome is a mechanical or electronic device that produces clicks or beeps that can be set to a specific tempo. Practicing with a metronome is very helpful because it helps you get a feel for playing in "perfect time."

Some musicians are afraid that a metronome will become a "crutch" if they practice with it. Like most things in life, moderation is the key. Don't have a metronome going every minute you practice. Use it when you are first learning something new so that you play it in perfect time right from the start. Use it to check rhythms and tempos periodically. But play without it, too, so you can make sure that your time is steady.

Some musicians also fear that practicing with a metronome will make their drumming sound "stiff." But good musicians do not become slaves to the metronome. They use it as a guide, and they avoid machine-like stiffness by letting some beats or time feels naturally fall just behind the metronome (laid back), putting others just ahead of the metronome (on top), and playing others right in sync (in the pocket).

Most recordings are made with a metronome (called a "click track") to guarantee that songs will not slow down or speed up. Using a click track also ensures that every take will be in exactly the same tempo, allowing the engineer to splice together different sections from different takes. So if you get used to practicing with a metronome, you will feel right at home when you go in the studio for the first time and they ask you to play to a click track.

Recorder

It's a great idea to record your practice sessions from time to time so you can sit back and listen to yourself. While we are actually playing, we might not notice that the tempo is speeding up or slowing down, or that something is stiff or sloppy. But listening back can reveal such things, and then we know what we need to go back and work on.

WARMING UP

Whether you are getting ready to practice in your bedroom or play a gig in front of 10,000 people, you should warm up first. The reason for warming up is to get the blood flowing into the muscles that you will be using for drumming so that you feel loose and relaxed. Therefore, you want to start out slow and easy. Don't try to force your hands to warm up by playing as fast as you can from the get-go. Start out with slow, relaxed, single strokes. Give the blood time to work its way down to the muscles that are starting to move.

The stiffer you feel at first, the more slowly you should play, and the more you should concentrate on relaxing your muscles so that the blood flow is not impeded. If you are about to play a gig in front of people, or play an audition, or perform in any situation that is causing you to be nervous or tense, *make yourself relax*. That tension will prevent the blood from lubricating your muscles, which will make your playing feel stiff, which will probably lead to even more tension. Don't sabotage yourself. Relax your muscles (and your mind!), play some slow, easy patterns on a pad, and let your body warm up.

Protect Your Ears

Drums and other percussion instruments can be very loud, and if your ears are exposed to loud sounds on a frequent basis, you can eventually suffer hearing damage. The first sign of potential ear damage is a ringing in the ears. At first, the ringing will usually go away after a couple of hours, but eventually it will be permanent—and there is no cure for hearing damage.

Therefore, you should wear headphones or use earplugs when you are going to be exposed to loud music. Many drummers suffer the greatest damage as a result of practicing drums in a small room, so when you practice at home, either use practice pads or wear hearing protection.

When practicing or performing with a band, most drummers prefer earplugs that cannot be seen. The inexpensive foam plugs that you can buy at most pharmacies will do the job, but they tend to muffle out the high frequencies, making the music sound muffled. Plugs are available that are specially designed for musicians, however. They muffle all of the frequencies evenly, so the effect is like turning down a volume control. These plugs are custom fitted to your ears, so contact an audiologist or visit a store that sells devices such as hearing aids for more information.

Once you are feeling relaxed, you can start playing faster, more difficult patterns. Many drummers use basic rhythm patterns for warm-ups as a way of "grounding" them before a gig or practice session. (Section 2 of this book includes some fundamental rhythm exercises that can be used as warm-ups.)

Warming up with a metronome is also a good idea. Start with a basic warm-up routine at a slow tempo. Once that feels relaxed and flowing, kick the metronome's tempo up a step and go through the routine again. Keep kicking the tempo up a step at a time until you feel totally ready to play. You will have warmed up your muscles and also exercised your timekeeping skills!

During their pre-performance warm-ups, drummers typically run through some of their trickier or more-demanding licks. That's fine, but make sure you are fully warmed up first, and don't confuse a warm-up session with a practice session. A warm-up *prepares* you to practice or play. Don't neglect that important part of the process!

Playing, Part 1

CHAPTER 4
HOLDING THE STICKS

What's Ahead:
- Matched grip
- Traditional grip
- Making the stroke

Most musicians are in direct physical contact with their instrument, holding it and playing it with their fingertips and/or lips. A few drums—such as congas, bongos, and djembes—are played directly with the hands, but most drums and percussion instruments are played by means of sticks or mallets. Therefore, it is crucial that these sticks and mallets become like part of your hands so that you can get every possible sound from your instruments, from explosive "whacks" on the drums to delicate colors on the cymbals.

There are two primary grips used by drummers: matched grip and traditional grip. The right-hand grip is identical with both grips; only the left-hand grip is different.

In the past, almost all drummers used traditional grip. But as rock music got louder and rock drummers needed more power, and when drumsets started getting bigger (requiring a longer reach to hit some of the drums and cymbals), many drummers switched to matched grip.

Today, many jazz drummers still use traditional grip because (1) they feel that traditional grip gives them a lighter touch, and (2) their kits tend to be smaller, and so they don't need the extra reach that matched grip provides. But both grips are valid, and while rock drummers are more likely to use matched grip and jazz drummers more likely to use traditional grip, you can find rock drummers using traditional and jazz drummers using matched. So ultimately you should go with the one that feels better to you and allows you maximum control.

MATCHED GRIP

Matched grip gets its name from the fact that both sticks are held the same way. Start by grasping the stick between the thumb and first finger about two-thirds of the distance between the tip of the stick and the butt end. Curl the remaining fingers under the stick, but do not press them tightly against the stick. Keep the hand relaxed.

The stick and the forearm should form a straight line.

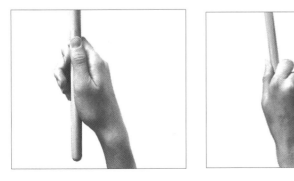

Position your snare drum and throne so that your forearms are angled down very slightly between the elbow and the wrist. Do not sit so low (or have the drum so high) that you have to hold your elbows up in order to play the snare drum. You will be hitting the snare drum a LOT, so you want your arms to be in a relaxed position when you are striking it. Your upper arms should hang straight down and be free of tension.

When you are striking the snare drum, the sticks should form about a 45 to 90 degree angle between each other as in the photo on the left.

TRADITIONAL GRIP

The right hand holds the stick the same way in traditional grip as it does in matched grip. For the left-hand grip, the stick is held tightly in the crevice between the thumb and palm. Curl the little finger and ring finger under the stick, so that the stick rests on the middle joint of the ring finger. Then curl the first and middle

fingers over the stick, but they should not clamp down on the stick. The stick is held between the thumb and hand, not between the fingers. The ring finger supports the weight of the stick when it is at rest. The first finger helps push the stick down when making a down-stroke.

Traditional grip was developed in order to accommodate a drum that was tilted as a result of being attached to a sling that is over the shoulder.

MAKING THE STROKE

Matched Grip – Both Hands

Concentrate on the wrist when making a stroke. Start with the stick several inches above the drum. With a quick, snapping motion of the wrist, bring the stick down. (The forearm will also move, but make sure the stroke is being made primarily by moving the wrist, not the elbow.) Keep the wrist relaxed so that as soon as the stick strikes the drumhead it can rebound off of it, as though the tip of the stick is a basketball that you are dribbling. Let the stick return to its starting position.

When you want a louder stroke, raise your stick higher—but the idea isn't to hit the drum *harder*, the idea is to hit the drum *faster*. Volume comes from velocity, so the reason for bringing the stick up higher is to give yourself room to attain more velocity, not to use more muscle.

Traditional Grip – Left Hand

To make the left-hand stroke with traditional grip, keep the wrist and forearm in a straight line, and twist the forearm quickly toward the drum, much like the motion you would use to turn a doorknob. The instant the stick hits the drumhead, let it rebound off the head and return to its starting position.

When striking a drum, the idea is for the stick to make the drumhead vibrate, not for the stick to have a collision with the drum! Having collisions can cause injury.

CHAPTER 5

READING MUSIC

What's Ahead:
* Why read music?
* Notation
* Pulse and meter
* Note and rest values
* Other time signatures
* Expression marks
* Other musical symbols

WHY READ MUSIC?

Must you learn how to read music in order to be a drummer? No. Plenty of drummers "play by ear" and do just fine. Then why would anyone bother learning to read music?

Because knowing how to read music can make playing music easier and more fun. If you know how to read music, you can learn how to play all kinds of great beats, grooves, and patterns by looking in drum books and drumming magazines. Do you want to learn a cool funk pattern, but you can't find anyone to show you how to play one? You can buy books that are full of funk grooves, and any other kind of groove you may ever want to learn.

You can probably find a note-by-note transcription of your favorite drum solo, too. Sure, you can learn it by listening to it over and over again on a CD, but can you really tell what's going on in that fast section? If you had it written out, you could understand every little note—not only the rhythms, but which drums they were played on.

Suppose you just joined a new band, and you have to learn three or four hour's worth of songs within a week or two. Being able to jot down the main beats and patterns for each song on a 3 x 5 card will help you learn the music faster, and you can even have those cards propped up where you can see them during the gig so you don't have to trust your memory with all that material.

Many playing opportunities require music reading. Professionals don't spend hours and hours rehearsing so they can learn everything by memory. They just run through the "charts" a couple of times and they've got it. Likewise, in the recording studio, time costs money, so they usually give the musicians written parts, and again, after a run-through or two, they are ready to record.

So reading music opens a lot of doors in terms of information you can draw from and opportunities you can take advantage of.

But having said all that, you need to develop your ears, too. In some bands, they have music for everyone except the drummer. Sometimes it's because they assume that drummers don't know how to read music, other times it's because the composer or arranger has no clue about how to write a drum chart, but often, it's because the drummer is expected to be able to play the appropriate beat just by hearing the song.

In other cases, the "chart" the drummer is given is what's called a "road map." It has the overall form of the tune so you know when to start, when to stop, when to repeat the chorus, and so on, but there are very few notes written in—just a few crucial hits or a generic beat to give you an idea of the overall feel. In such a case, you have to use a combination of reading and listening to come up with the drum part.

So along with learning new rhythms and grooves from drum books and drum magazines, spend some time just listening to music and trying to figure out what the drummer is doing. The best drummers are good readers with good ears. Those are the drummers that can cover any situation.

NOTATION

Music reading is often made out to be a big mystery, or something that is incredibly difficult. Wrong! And reading drum music is even easier than reading music for other instruments because we don't have all the different pitches, scales, and key signatures. For the most part, we are just reading rhythmic notation, which is only a portion of what other instrumentalists have to deal with.

Let's start with some basics. Like other instruments, drums are generally written on a five-line staff.

With other instruments, each line and space represents a different pitch, but for drummers, each line or space represents a different part of the drumset. At the very beginning of a staff, you will see a clef, which helps you determine what type of instrument the music is written for. Instruments such as guitar, trumpet, and clarinet use treble clef. Instruments such as bass and tuba use bass clef. A piano uses a grand staff with treble clef on top and bass clef on the bottom.

Treble and bass clefs let the players know that specific lines and spaces on the staff represent specific pitches. But since drums don't have specific pitches, and not everyone arranges the different parts of the drumset on a staff the same way, drum music is usually written on a staff with a *rhythm clef*. You might see some different versions of the rhythm clef.

Since not everyone notates drums exactly the same way, there is usually a "key" or "legend" that will guide you. The following example shows the notation system adapted by the *Percussive Arts Society*, which is used by most major music publishers. (This notation key can be expanded to include additional drums and cymbals, as seen on the reference sheet at the end of the book, but for now we'll just show the most standard arrangement.)

Notice that the cymbals have "X" noteheads, and the drums have regular noteheads. Also, the instruments are arranged on the staff in somewhat the same way that they are set up: instruments that you play with your feet (bass drum and hi-hat pedals) are at the bottom, the drums that are generally right in front of you (snare drum, toms) are in the middle of the staff, and the cymbals that are mounted above the toms on stands are at the top of the staff.

PULSE AND METER

Back in the 1950s and '60s, a TV show called *American Bandstand*, hosted by Dick Clark, had a regular feature in which a panel of teenagers rated new records. One of the most common phrases used by these reviewers was, "This record has a good beat that I could dance to."

When most people refer to the "beat," they are talking about the underlying pulse that exists in all music—whether it's a hip-hop song or a Beethoven symphony. Just like the pulse of your heartbeat, the musical "pulse" chugs along and gives a tune momentum. If you have ever tapped your foot, danced, or clapped your hands to music, you were locking in with the pulse.

Many people use the terms "pulse" and "beat" to mean the same thing. But when drummers talk about playing a particular "beat," they are usually referring to the specific pattern they are playing for a particular song. In drummers' language, two songs could have the same pulse but have different "beats."

The pulse of a song is generally reflected by the bottom number of its time signature, which is the pair of numbers, one above the other, that appear at the beginning of every piece of music. The time signature defines the song's meter. Here are some examples:

4/4 time   3/4 time   2/4 time   6/8 time   5/8 time   12/8 time   7/16 time

The bottom number represents the type of note that gets one beat, or that forms the pulse. A "2" represents a half note; a "4" represents a quarter note; an "8" represents an eighth note; a "16" represents a sixteenth note. (It's theoretically possible to have a "1" representing a whole note, a "32" representing a thirty-second note, a "64" representing a sixty-fourth note, and so on, but you will seldom, if ever, encounter time signatures with those numbers on the bottom.)

The top number tells you how many beats are in each measure. What is a measure? *Measures* are the individual units within a staff, delimited by *bar lines*. (A measure can also be called a *bar*.)

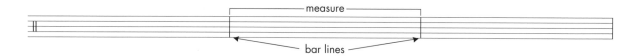

When playing "popular" music (rock, jazz, blues, country, etc.), the time signature you will encounter most often is 4/4. Sometimes, however, instead of seeing a 4/4 time signature at the beginning of a piece, you will see this: This is called the "common time" signature and is exactly the same as 4/4 time.

Music exists in time, so we use measures, beats, and different note values to organize and subdivide that time, just as we organize "real" time into hours, minutes, and seconds.

So, 4/4 literally means four quarter notes per measure. Is that all you can have in a measure? Not at all! (That would be pretty boring music.) It just means that, for example, in 4/4 time, the basic pulse is made up of quarter notes, and that no matter what kind of rhythm patterns you play in a measure, the sum of all the note values will be equal to four quarter notes.

We'll discuss other time signatures later in this section, but for now let's stay with 4/4 and look at individual note values.

NOTE AND REST VALUES

Now we get into some math—but it's pretty simple. In 4/4 time, as we've already discussed, a quarter note gets one beat. We can double the quarter note, giving us a *half note*, which is worth two beats (1/4 + 1/4 = 1/2). A *whole note* is worth four beats.

Going the other direction, we can split quarter notes in half, giving us *eighth notes*. Splitting eighth notes in half gives us *sixteenth notes*. Sixteenth notes can be divided in half to form *thirty-second notes*, which can be cut in half to form *sixty-fourth notes*, and so on. (You will seldom see thirty-second notes, and sixty-fourth notes are pretty rare in most pop music.)

The following chart shows the different note values that you are most likely to encounter, and how they are counted in 4/4 time.

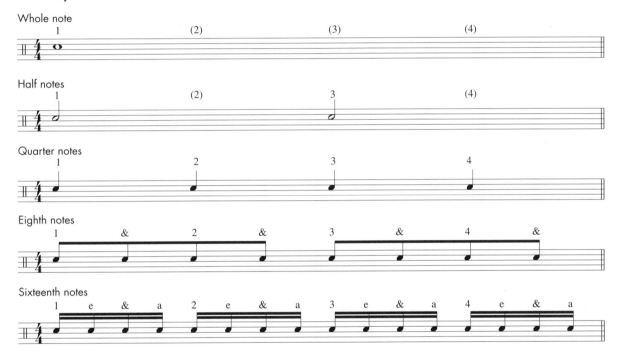

Rests

Each note has a corresponding rest that can be used as a "place holder," so to speak.

Whole rest   Half rest   Quarter rest   Eighth rest   Sixteenth rest

Triplets and Tuplets

As we've seen, eighth notes divide a quarter note in half, and sixteenth notes divide an eighth note in half or divide a quarter note into fourths. If we want to divide a note into thirds, we use a *triplet*, which consists of three notes played in the space of two notes. Triplets are indicated with a small 3 over beamed notes and a 3 with a bracket over non-beamed notes. Any note values can be grouped as triplets.

Three eighth notes in the space of two eighth notes:

Three sixteenth notes in the space of two sixteenth notes:

Three quarter notes in the space of two quarter notes:

Three half notes in the space of two half notes:

Within a triplet, the usual relationships between note values exists, so if you only want the first and third note of a triplet, you can substitute a rest for the second note, or you can use a longer note value for the first note:

Triplets are just one type of *tuplet*, which is any group of notes that, instead of following normal subdivision rules (as defined by the meter), consists of more (or fewer) notes of equal value.

Quintuplet: 5 notes in the space of 4 regular notes of the same value.

Sextuplet: 6 notes in the space of 4 regular notes of the same value.

A sextuplet can also be thought of as a pair of triplets.

Septuplet: 7 notes in the space of 4 regular notes of the same value.

Duplet: 2 notes in the space of three regular notes of the same value. This would normally occur in a meter such as 6/8, where each main beat is normally understood to be divisible by three—in contradistinction to the duple division of main beats in, for example, 4/4. (More about this meter shortly).

Dotted Notes

When a dot is added after a note, the note's value increases by one half. For example, we know that (in 4/4 time) a half note is worth two beats, so a dotted-half is worth three beats. A quarter note is worth one beat; a dotted-quarter is worth one-and-a-half beats. An eighth note is worth half a beat; a dotted-eighth is worth three-fourths of a beat. Here are some examples:

OTHER TIME SIGNATURES

Quarter Time

Although much pop music is written in 4/4 time, there are other time signatures in which the quarter note gets the beat. One that turns up quite a bit is 3/4, which is sometimes called "waltz time" because it is the time signature used for this popular ballroom dance. In 3/4 time, there are only three beats to a measure, but the note values have the same relationships that they have in 4/4 time. (Thus, you can't have a whole note in 3/4 time because there isn't room. A whole note takes up four beats, and we only have room for three beats per measure.)

Other quarter-time signatures you might encounter are 2/4, 5/4, 6/4, and 7/4. You can put just about any number on top, but generally those numbers don't get too large.

Eighth Time

If the time signature has an 8 on the bottom, then the eighth note gets the beat: that is, each eighth note gets a count. Thus, a quarter note gets two counts (like a half note did in 4/4); a half note gets four counts; a whole note gets eight counts; sixteenth notes get a half count each; and thirty-second notes get one-fourth of a count a piece.

One of the most widely used time signatures in eighth time is 6/8, which consists of six eighth notes (or a combination of notes that equals six eighth notes) per measure. In math, 3/4 and 6/8 are considered equal, and in music, both time signatures have the same number of eighth notes per measure. But there is a big difference in the way the two time signatures are felt and conceived. In 3/4 time, there are three main beats (the quarters), and eighth notes are usually grouped in pairs. But in 6/8, the eighth notes are usually beamed in groups of three, reflecting the fact that 6/8 is generally felt "in two," with two main beats—the 1 and the 4, which is equivalent to two dotted-quarter note beats. So even though 6/8 is mathematically the same as 3/4, it sounds more like 2/4 with triplets.

The following chart shows how the note values would be counted in 6/8 time.

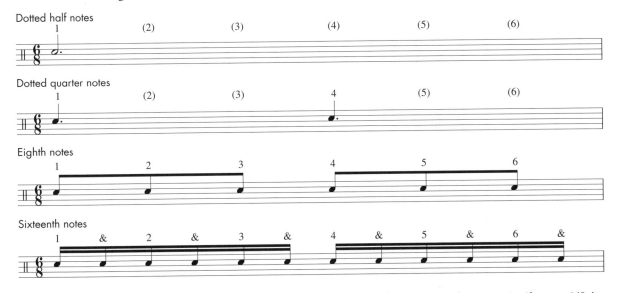

Eighth-based time signatures that have a 3, 9, or 12 as the top number are similar to 6/8 in the respect that the eighth notes are usually grouped in threes, and dotted quarter notes are considered the main beats.

Often 6/8 is counted "in two," 9/8 is counted "in three," and 12/8 is counted "in four."

Cut-time

A related symbol to common time is the cut-time signature, which looks like this:
Cut-time is notated the same as 4/4 time, but every note value is cut in half so that,
for example, a half note gets one beat (instead of two), a quarter note gets a half
beat (instead of a full beat), an eighth note gets one-fourth beat (instead of a half beat), and so on.
The following chart shows how basic note values are counted in cut-time.

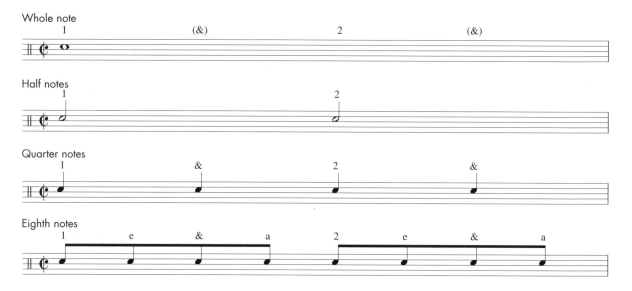

Essentially, cut-time is the same as 2/2 time, where the half note gets the beat, a quarter note gets half a beat, and so on.

Odd Times

Although some people consider any time signature with an "odd" number on the top to be an "odd time" signature, many people don't categorize time signatures with a 3 or 9 as the top number as "odd," because the notes tend to be felt in consistent groups of three, giving the overall pulse a very "even" feel.

Rather, "odd times" are usually signatures with numbers such as 5 or 7 in the top position. Generally, such time signatures are divided into "long" and "short" beats. For example, 5/4 and 5/8 are generally thought of as 2 + 3 or 3 + 2, in terms of where the "main" beats are. When playing drumset, these are the beats on which the bass drum would most likely play.

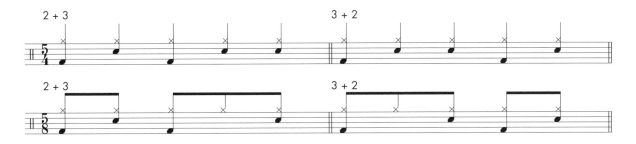

A 7/4 or 7/8 time signature could be divided three ways: 2 + 2 + 3, 2 + 3 + 2, or 3 + 2 + 2.

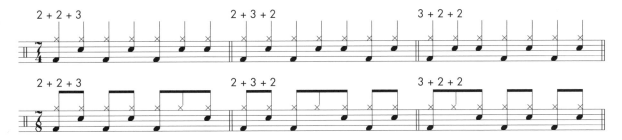

A lot of people used to think that odd times didn't "swing" or "groove," but countless musicians have proven that theory wrong. (Check out Joe Morello's swinging 5/4 groove on "Take Five" by the Dave Brubeck Quartet.)

EXPRESSION MARKS

Dynamics

Dynamics have to do with how loudly or softly you are playing. There's an old joke about a drummer saying, "Whaddya mean use more dynamics? I'm playing as loud as I can!" Remember, the best music doesn't maintain the same volume all the way through. Being loud all the time wears listeners out. You need to be soft sometimes, saving the really loud playing for climactic moments.

The two most important dynamics are f and p. The f stands for *forte*, which means *loud*. The p stands for *piano*, which means *soft*. The more f's you have, the louder the dynamic; the more p's you have, the softer the dynamic. In between f and p are *mf* and *mp*. The m stands for *mezzo*, which means *medium*. So *mf* (*mezzo forte*) is *medium loud* and *mp* (*mezzo piano*) is *medium soft*.

Here is a chart showing the dynamic range. Sometimes, for dramatic effect, an arranger might mark something with more than three p's to indicate extremely soft, or more than three f's to indicate RIDICULOUSLY LOUD. But these are the ones you will usually see.

fff	=	*fortissississimo*	=	loudest
ff	=	*fortissimo*	=	louder
f	=	*forte*	=	loud
mf	=	*mezzo forte*	=	medium loud
mp	=	*mezzo piano*	=	medium soft
p	=	*piano*	=	soft
pp	=	*pianissimo*	=	softer
ppp	=	*pianississimo*	=	softest

If you see a note marked *sf* or *sfz*, this indicates a heavily accented note. Sometimes you might see *fp*, which is pronounced *forte-piano*, and means to make a loud "attack" immediately followed by softer playing.

Dynamics are *relative*, which means that a certain dynamic marking does not always suggest the same volume. You have to take into account who you are playing with, and where you are playing. For example, if you are playing with an electrified heavy metal band in an arena, *forte* is going to be a lot louder than if you are playing in a small club with an acoustic piano and an acoustic bass. So no matter how the music is marked, use your ears and play at a volume that is appropriate to the situation.

Accents

An accent is a mark placed over or under a note to indicate that only that note should be louder:

You'll notice that an accent mark looks like a "greater than" symbol in math. In terms of dynamics, that's exactly what it means. An accented note has a volume that is greater than whatever dynamic you are currently in.

Some drummers think that an accent means you should hit the note as hard as possible. Not true (unless the dynamic is *fff*). The accented note is a little louder than whatever dynamic you are already in, so an accented note in a *piano* section will not be as loud as an accented note in a *forte* section.

Crescendos and Diminuendos

If the music is supposed to gradually get louder, it will be marked with a *crescendo*. There are two ways a *crescendo* may be indicated. If it covers just a few notes, you will usually see this symbol (sometimes called a "hairpin *crescendo*"): ⬍

If it extends over a larger area, you will usually see the abbreviation *cresc.* under the music, along with a dotted line letting you know how long the *crescendo* lasts.

If the music is supposed to get softer gradually, it will be marked with a *diminuendo*. Again, there are two ways it can be marked. If it covers just a few notes, you will usually see this symbol (sometimes called a "hairpin *diminuendo*"): ⬎

If it extends over a larger area, you will usually see the abbreviation *dim.* under the music, along with a dotted line letting you know how long the *diminuendo* lasts. You might also see *decresc.*, an abbreviation for *decrescendo* (the opposite of crescendo), which means the same thing as *diminuendo*.

A *crescendo* or *diminuendo* should always lead to a new dynamic marking. Look ahead to see how loud or soft you are ultimately supposed to get so that you can pace yourself and not get to loud or too soft too soon.

OTHER MUSICAL SYMBOLS
Repeats

In most music, some things get played more than once. It might be a measure or two, or it might be a very large section. In order to maximize the efficiency of the notation, which helps prevent having to turn a lot of pages when you are playing, composers and arrangers use various repeat signs.

The first one we'll look at is a single-measure repeat.

When you see this symbol, play whatever you played in the previous measure again. You can have lots of single-measure repeats in a row, indicating that you play the same bar over and over. Drummers see a lot of these, because we are often playing a repetitive groove. So, if you see this:

...play this:

There is also a symbol that means to play the previous *two* measures again:

This does NOT mean to play the preceding measure twice; it means to go back two measures and play each one once. In other words, if you see this:

...play this:

If more than two measures are to be repeated, repeat dots are used. They come in pairs that look like this:

When you see those, you repeat whatever is between the two sets of dots. It might be three or four measures, or it might be a whole chorus of a song.

First and Second Endings

Sometimes, everything in a large section of music will be repeated except the last couple of measures. Rather than rewrite the entire section for the sake of those one or two measures, arrangers will use *1st* and *2nd endings*. Look at the following example:

In the example above, you would play measures 1 through 8, then repeat back to measure one. Then, after you play measure 7, you would skip measure 8 (which is the first ending) and play measure 9, which is the second ending.

Slashes

Sometimes, a drum chart will have slashes in several measures, which look like this:

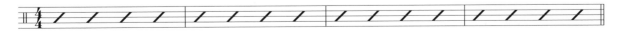

The slashes generally indicate that you are to continue in the style of the tune, but that you have a certain amount of freedom to play whatever you feel is appropriate. Sometimes, the basic groove will be written out, but slashes will be used for fills and solos so that you can improvise whatever you want. Other times, slashes are used to indicate that you are supposed to keep time. In some cases, slashes are used for just about everything. (See the sample drum chart later in the next section)

D.S., D.C., Sign, Fine, and Coda

There are a few other "directional" signals you need to know about. At some point in a piece you might see the letters D.S. or D.C. D.S. stands for *dal Segno* (Italian for "from the sign"), which means to go back to the "sign," which looks like this: 𝄋. You then start playing from there. Instead of D.S., you might see D.C., which stands for *da Capo* ("from the top") and means that you are to go back to the very beginning.

A *D.C.* or *D.S.* is usually accompanied by *al Fine* or *al Coda*. An *al Fine* means "to the end," and it means to play until you reach the *Fine* marking. (*Fine* is Italian for "end" or "final.") An *al Coda* means "to the Coda," with the *Coda* (Italian for "tail") being a section at the very end of a piece. So you will go back to the beginning (D.C.) or to the Sign (D.S.), and play until you get to a symbol that looks like this: ⊕. Then you jump to the *Coda*, which will have the same Coda sign (⊕) and the word "Coda," and finish out the piece.

It is important for all musicians to understand these various directions so they don't get lost in the music. But it is especially important for drummers, because sometimes the "chart" or "road map" we are given has very little music, just a lot of "directional symbols" to help us understand the structure of a tune. A typical drum chart might look like this:

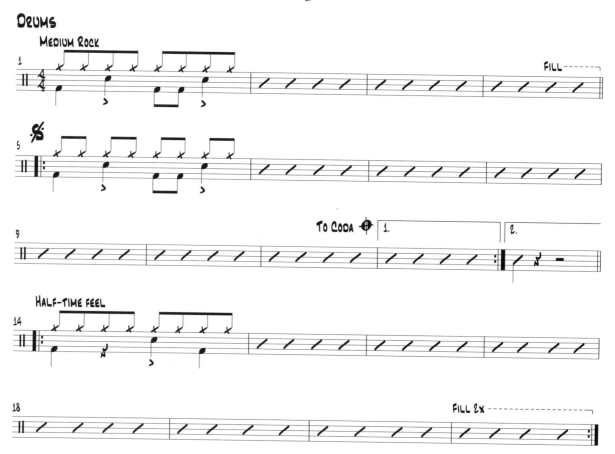

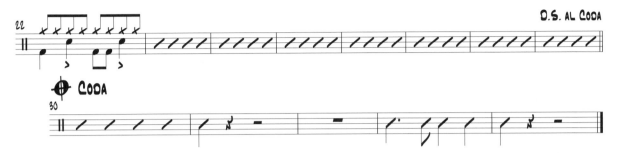

In this chart, you are told that the piece is played in a Medium Rock feel, which means the tempo is not too fast or too slow. The beat that is given in the first bar is just a general guideline. You might start with that, but use your ears, and feel free to add variations that fit with the music. The slashes indicate that you should continue in the same style. In measure 4, there is an indication that you should play a *fill* (short bridging "solo") during beats 3 and 4. You can play whatever you want, as long as it fits the music!

At the beginning of the next section, there are repeat dots, telling you that this section will be played twice. You also see the "Sign" (𝄋) at the beginning of measure 5, up above the staff. Remember where you saw it; you'll need to come back to it later.

Play measures 5 through 11, and then play measure 12, which is the 1st ending. You see repeat dots at the end of measure 12, so go back to measure 5 and play measures 5 through 11 again, but this time skip measure 12 (the 1st ending) and play measure 13 (the second ending).

You'll notice that there is just one note at the beginning of measure 13, written with a slash notehead. That tells you to rest after you play a note on beat one, but it's up to you how you play that note. Again, use your ears. It might call for a cymbal crash, it might sound best with just a bass-drum note, or it might be played with a combination of drums and cymbals. The chart is just letting you know that the drums should only play the first beat, and then lay out for the rest of the measure.

The next section (measure 14), which also has repeat dots, has an indication that this should be played with a half-time feel. A basic half-time pattern is notated as a guide, but you don't necessarily have to play *only* what is written if you can come up with a half-time groove that sounds better. At the end of this repeated section (measure 21), you see the words "fill 2X." That means you should play a fill the "second time" you play that section. (If you were supposed to play a fill both times, it would just say "fill.")

After repeating the half-time section, notes are written in measure 22 indicating a return to the original feel. At the end of this section, you see "D.S. al Coda." Remember that "Sign" you saw in measure 5? Go back there and play that section again. But at the end of measure 11 you see the Coda sign, so you immediately jump to the Coda at the bottom of the chart. You continue the groove for one measure, stopping on the downbeat of measure 31. Then you have seven beats of rest, which is most likely a solo for the singer or one of the other instrumentalists.

The last two bars have rhythm cues. Again, they are not telling you exactly what to play; the notes are just telling you what the main accents are. Very likely, the whole band is playing this rhythm together. You can play just the notes that are indicated, on whatever drums or cymbals you think are appropriate, or you can also play notes in between the written notes, making sure that the written notes are accented. (For example, you might play a bass drum/crash cymbal combination on the written notes and fill in between those notes with snare drum or tom-tom hits. As always, use your ears.)

The first time through a chart, play very simply. You might play the rhythms exactly as written so you can devote most of your attention to listening to what the rest of the musicians are doing. Then, the next time you play it, you'll have a better idea of what you can do to make the drum part more interesting.

CHAPTER 6

PLAYING WITH THE HANDS AND FEET

What's Ahead:
- Playing the snare drum
- Playing snare drum with ride cymbal or hi-hat
- Playing with the feet

PLAYING SNARE DRUM

Now that we've got all that math and theory out of the way, let's start playing! We'll start with some fundamental rhythm patterns in 4/4 time, played just on the snare drum with the hands. This will give you an understanding of basic rhythm patterns that will be applied to full drumset, and these one-drum patterns are also used in playing fills and solos (see Chapter 9).

Sticking

The word "sticking" refers to which hand you use to play which note. There are a couple of different sticking systems that drummers typically use.

Alternating

With the "alternating" method of sticking, you basically go back and forth between right hand and left hand. This is essentially the basis of rudimental sticking, except that rudimental sticking has a lot of double strokes. (See Chapter 24, "Rudiments.") The idea is that whatever you can play with your right hand, you should be able to play with your left. Those who use alternating sticking contend that it helps make their hands more equal and gives them more freedom in their playing.

Right-hand Lead

Also known as the "Straight system" (named after Edward B. Straight, who invented it), right-hand lead is based on playing "strong" beats with the right hand and "weak" beats with the left. The idea is that your playing is more consistent, because you will always play the same rhythm with the same sticking pattern.

Which to Use?

Either sticking method is valid, but if you are mostly going to be playing drumset, in which the right and left hands are often playing independent parts (one hand on the ride cymbal and the other on the snare drum), the only time the sticking will become an issue is when you are doing fills and solos. Because you will be playing on more than one drum, it makes most sense to use alternating sticking, because that will give you more freedom to go in either direction around the kit.

In the following rhythms, alternating sticking is indicated under the notes. But these are just suggestions, not rules. All that really matters is that you sound good, so use the sticking method that gives you the best sound and most control.

Don't become a "one-handed" drummer—one who has a great right hand that plays all the important notes, but whose left hand is very weak. Work to develop both of your hands equally.

Here are some basic patterns using whole notes, half notes, and quarter notes in 4/4 time, with counting indicated over the notes and sticking indicated under the notes. (*R* = right hand; *L* = left hand.)

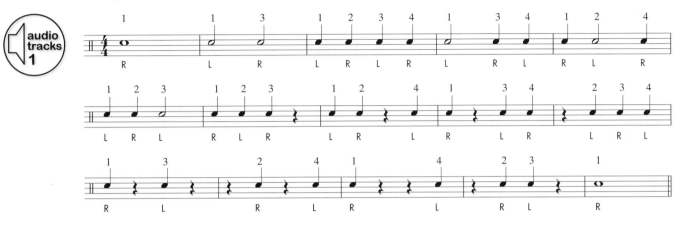

The following example combines quarters and eighths into some common patterns:

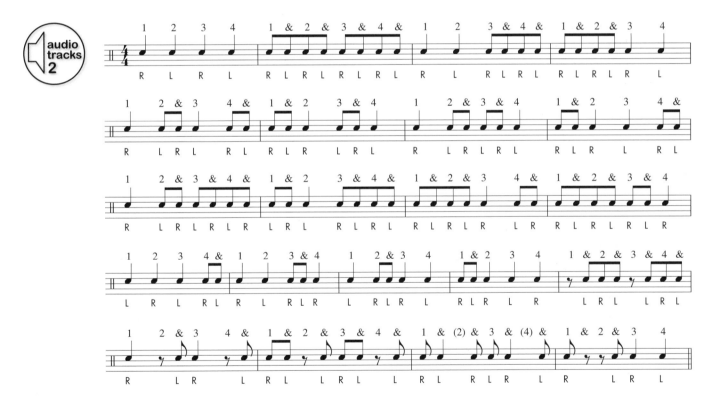

Here are some very basic rhythm patterns using quarters, eighths, and sixteenths. Recognizing rhythm patterns, rather than just seeing individual notes, is like reading words and sentences instead of individual letters.

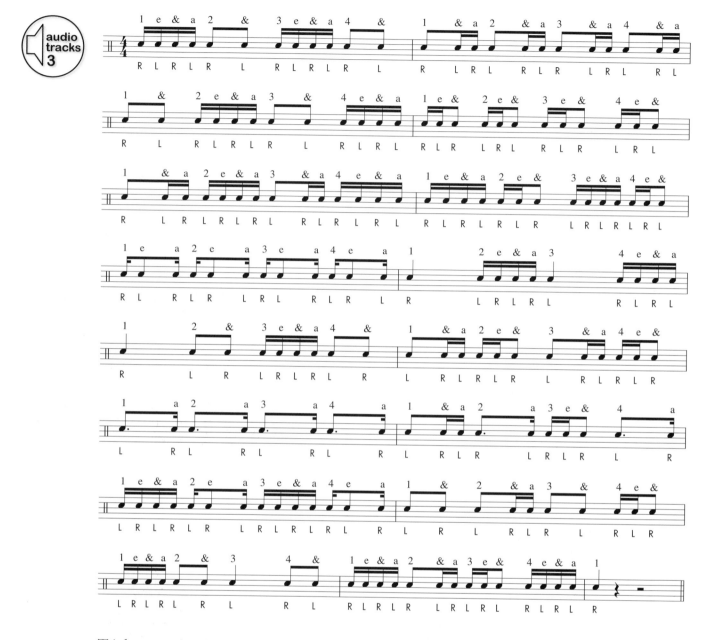

Triplet counting is not as standardized as the counting of "regular" notes. One way to count triplets is "1 and a 2 and a" etc., but this can be confused with the method for counting sixteenth notes:

Another way is to use the regular number or syllable that the triplet begins on and count the second and third notes with the syllables "trip" and "let." (In the following example, "trip" will be represented with a "T" and "let" with an "L.")

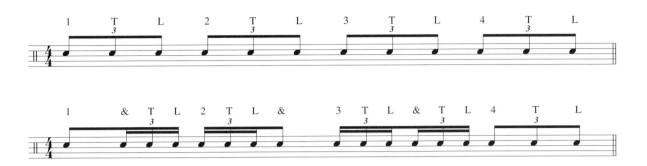

PLAYING SNARE DRUM WITH RIDE CYMBAL OR HI-HAT

Most of the time, when we're playing drumset, each hand is playing a different instrument. Generally, one hand will be riding on the ride cymbal or closed hi-hat while the other hand is playing snare drum.

Playing "open handed"

Most drummers do all of their riding, whether it's on the ride cymbal or the hi-hat, with their right hand, and they play the snare drum with the left. If they use a standard setup, that means when they are playing ride cymbal, their arms are in a natural, "open" position, with the right hand playing a cymbal on the right side of the kit, and the left hand playing a snare drum that is to the left of the kit.

But when they switch from ride cymbal to hi-hat, they cross their right hand over their left hand. There is certainly nothing wrong with doing this; countless drummers have proven that it works fine.

But there is another way, which may be worth experimenting with, especially if you are just starting out and haven't developed any particular habits yet. The other way is to play "open handed." That means that you still play the ride cymbal with your right hand and the snare with the left. But when you are riding on the hi-hat, you play hi-hat with the left hand, and snare drum with the right. (Of course, this assumes that you are using matched grip. Riding on the hi-hat with a left-hand traditional grip would be awkward.)

Learning to ride with either hand does wonders for your coordination. Riding on the hi-hat with your left hand also makes it easier to play loud backbeats on the snare drum with your right hand.

Playing two different instruments and patterns at the same time is not as difficult as many people seem to think. It's just a matter of seeing how the hands work together, and there are only three choices: the right hand plays by itself; the left hand plays by itself; both hands play together.

Here is one of the most frequently used hand patterns in all of drumset playing. One hand (usually the right) plays eighth notes on either the ride cymbal or closed hi-hat, while the other hand plays backbeats on the snare drum.

At first, you might find yourself stopping the right hand while the left hand hits. So concentrate on making both hands hit together. When working with beginning students, I sometimes have them say this while they are first attempting this pattern:

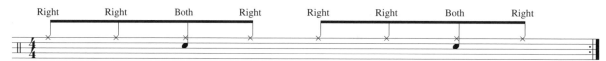

Once you get that happening, try some other snare drum patterns with the eighth-note ride.

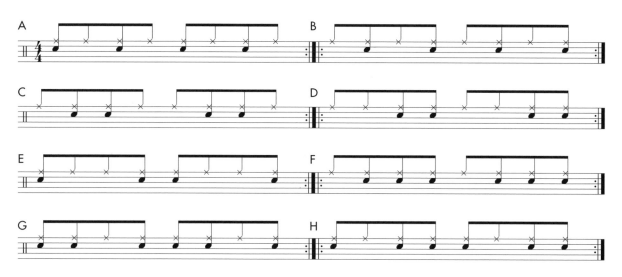

Now let's change the ride pattern to quarter notes.

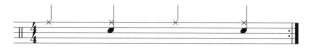

We can play snare drum notes in between the ride notes, just as we previously played cymbal notes in between snare notes. But some cymbal notes will not have snare notes in between them, so in the following patterns, be sure to count very carefully so that the quarter-note ride stays perfectly even. (You might want to use a metronome.)

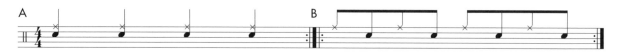

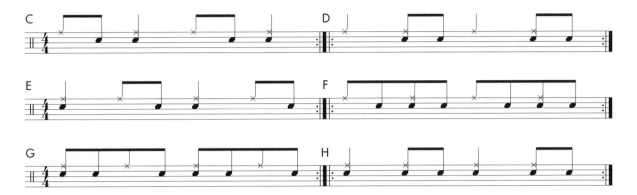

Let's practice some basic right-hand/left-hand coordination with other rhythm feels. Here are some patterns with triplets.

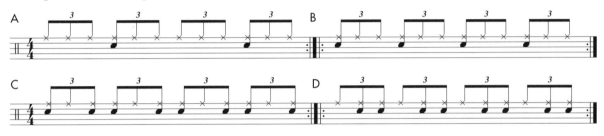

Here are some shuffle patterns.

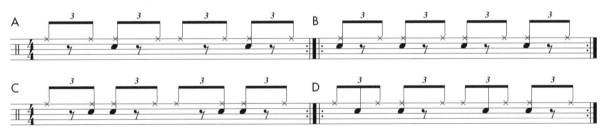

Here are some sixteenth-note patterns.

These, of course, are only a few of the possibilities, but they will get you started.

PLAYING WITH THE FEET
Bass Drum
When making the bass drum stroke, you need to "ride" the pedal. In other words, let the pedal's spring do its job of getting the beater back and away from the drumhead as soon as the stroke is made. Don't drive the beater into the head and leave it there. That will break a lot of drumheads (and bass drum heads are expensive) and can also cause injury to your leg and ankle muscles.

Some drummers just have their toes on the pedal and their heels up, and they make the stroke primarily with a leg motion. This is usually done for volume and power. Other drummers keep their foot flat on the pedal and make the stroke from the ankle. This is a good way to play softer. The best drummers use both techniques depending on how loud the stroke should be. Experiment with both so that you can get a full range of dynamics.

Hi-hat
When playing the hi-hat with the foot, we do just the opposite of what we did with the bass drum stroke. You want to bring the two cymbals together quickly and solidly so that they make a "chick" sound. But then you need to hold your foot down briefly. If you bring it up as soon as the cymbals strike each other, instead of a "chick" you'll get a crash (referred to as a hi-hat "splash"). Now and then you might do that for a special effect, but generally you want that dry "chick" sound, so keep your foot down on the pedal until just before you need to play another hi-hat note.

Often, when drummers ride on the closed hi-hat cymbals, they will open the cymbals on selected notes, getting sort of a "swoosh" sound. These notes are sometimes referred to as hi-hat "barks." An open hi-hat note is generally indicated with a small "o" over the note, as shown on the "&" of 3 in the following example.

In the above example, you would raise your left foot on the "&" of 3 as you are striking the note with your riding hand, and then you would bring your foot back down on beat 4. (The "+" sign indicates a "closed hi-hat.")

Coordinating Bass Drum and Hi-hat
Generally, the bass drum works with the snare drum to define the "beat," or main rhythm pattern of a song, while the hi-hat works with the ride cymbal to define the overall feel or pulse. If you are riding on a closed hi-hat, then the pedal won't be used at all (except occasionally to open the cymbals for an effect: See Chapters 21 and 23).

In some of the most basic drumset beats, the bass drum plays on 1 and 3, while the hi-hat plays on 2 and 4.

A similar pattern (used in a lot of dance music) involves the bass drum keeping a straight quarter-note pulse (often referred to as playing "four on the floor").

Here are some other bass drum variations with the hi-hat maintaining a 2 and 4 backbeat.

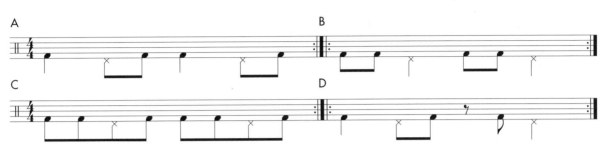

The hi-hat part is usually pretty consistent, working in conjunction with the ride cymbal. In addition to playing backbeats, sometimes the hi-hat keeps a straight quarter-note pulse as in the following patterns.

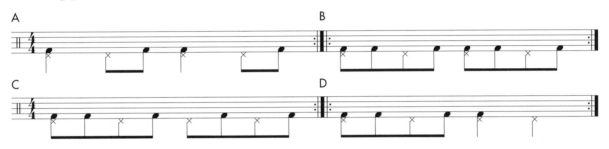

Other times, the hi-hat plays upbeats, as in the following bass drum/hi-hat patterns:

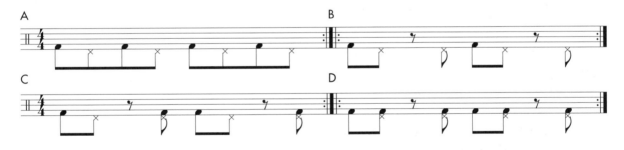

Double Bass Drum

If you have two bass drums, or a double bass drum pedal, you will often be playing the same kinds of rhythms between your two feet that you might play on a snare drum with your two hands. To develop the coordination, go back to the snare drum patterns at the beginning of this chapter and try playing them between your two feet.

For more on double bass drumming, see Chapter 13.

CHAPTER 7

MULTI-LIMB PLAYING

What's Ahead:

- Time and feel
- Combining the limbs

TIME AND FEEL

As drummers, one of our primary responsibilities is to define the pulse, or to keep the "time." Often, we will be playing more than one layer of time in the course of playing a "beat." This leads to yet another word drummers use, which is "feel." That word can be used to refer in very general terms to a drummer's general style, and people will talk about a drummer having a solid feel, a loose feel, a stiff feel (not good!), a laid-back feel, and so on. But in more technical terms, the word "feel" is often used to define the way the pulse is being subdivided.

The following is a very basic 4/4 "beat," with the bass drum defining the quarter-note pulse and the snare drum reinforcing the backbeats.

audio tracks 4

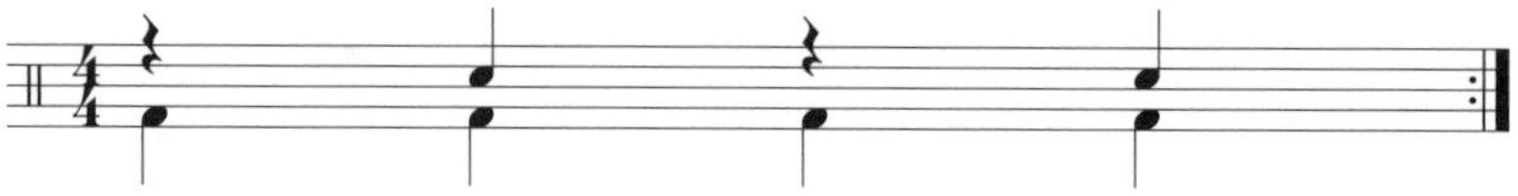

By altering the hi-hat or ride-cymbal pattern, you can give that basic beat a variety of "feels" to accommodate a variety of song styles. For a hard rock song, the feel and the beat might both be quarter notes.

audio tracks 5

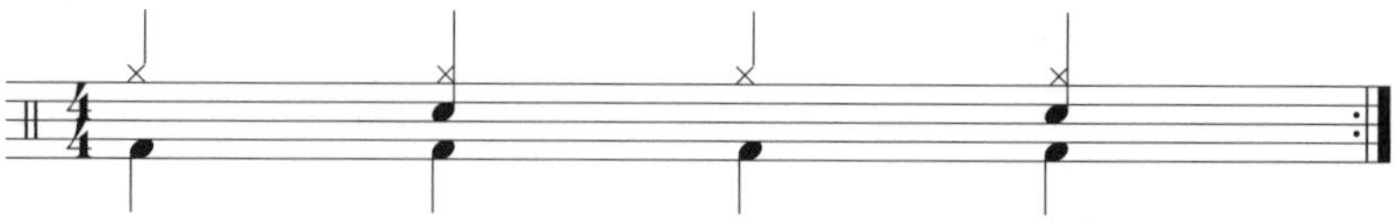

For a pop song, you might play that beat with an eighth-note feel.

audio tracks 6

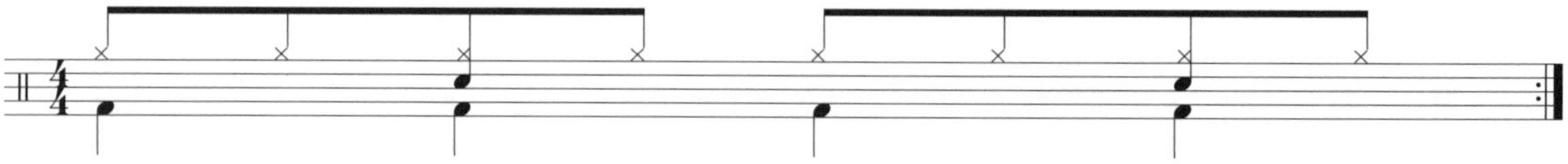

How about a swinging jazz feel?

audio tracks 7

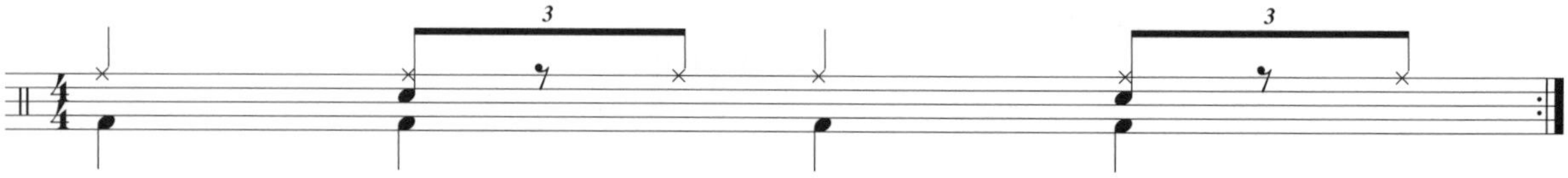

Let's try a sixteenth-note feel.

audio tracks 8

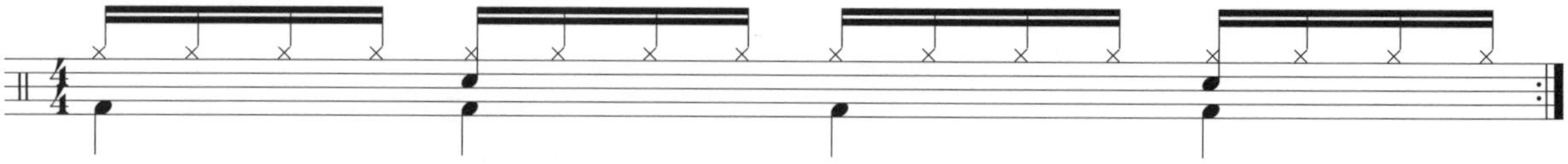

Of course, there are a lot of other notes you can play on the bass and snare drums within each of those styles. And you would also alter the sound of the different parts of the kit, depending on the style. For example, with the rock styles, the bass and snare drums would be very loud and aggressive. With jazz, the ride cymbal would be the dominant voice, and the bass drum would be played very softly. But these simple examples serve to illustrate the relationship between the beat, the pulse, and the feel. All of the previous examples have the same 4/4 pulse, and in these examples, they are each being played with the same beat. Yet, each has a different *feel*.

Not every drumset pattern separates the beat and feel to that extent. Often the bass drum, ride cymbal or hi-hat, and snare drum work together to define the beat, and the feel is implied by the overall sound, rather than by what is played on a single component of the drumkit. We'll explore some of the different patterns that can be played within each style in Section 4.

COMBINING THE LIMBS

Let's start combining limbs and different parts of the drumset to create grooves and feels. It's best to start out with different combinations of limbs so that you can isolate the techniques involved, and also understand how the different limbs work together.

Quarter-note Feel

Here is a very basic pattern made up just of quarter notes.

If you are new to drumset coordination, you should first practice this pattern in parts. You might even want to start with one instrument/limb at a time. For example, play along with the track with just the right hand on the ride cymbal. Then play along with just the left hand on the snare drum. Play along again with just the right foot on bass drum, and then go through it once more with just the left foot on the hi-hat pedal.

Now play along using pairs of instruments. Start with just the hands: right hand on ride cymbal, and left hand on snare drum. Then play through the track with just the feet: right foot on bass drum, left foot on hi-hat.

Now start mixing the limbs: ride cymbal and bass drum; snare drum and hi-hat; ride cymbal and hi-hat; bass drum and snare drum.

Then try all the combinations of three instruments: ride cymbal, snare drum, bass drum; ride cymbal, snare drum, hi-hat; ride cymbal, bass drum, hi-hat; bass drum, snare drum, hi-hat.

Finally, put them all together.

As a contrast to riding on the cymbal, you can instead ride on a closed hi-hat. When you do that, keep your foot down on the hi-hat pedal.

Eighth-note Feel

Here is a very fundamental pattern with an eighth-note ride that can be played along with the CD. You will notice that there are mostly quarter notes in the other instruments, except for two eighth notes in the bass drum part. You might want to start by playing combinations of two instruments (snare and ride, bass drum and hi-hat, bass drum and snare, etc.), then move on to combinations of three instruments, and finally play the entire pattern.

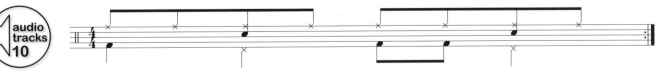

Alternatively, you could ride on a closed hi-hat, leaving out the "hi-hat with foot" part.

Next, we'll take the previous pattern and substitute a quarter-note ride for the eighth-note ride. This means that the bass drum note that is on the "&" of 3 will be played by itself. At first, count straight eighth notes while you are playing so that you place each note accurately.

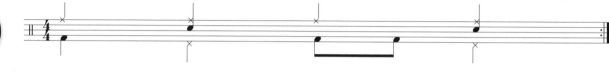

Sixteenth-note Feel

Here are two very fundamental patterns with a sixteenth-note ride. The first one is designed for slow to medium tempos and involves playing all of the sixteenths with one hand.

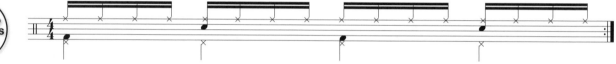

When playing a sixteenth-note ride on the closed hi-hat at medium to fast tempos, drummers will typically alternate the hands, coming off the hi-hat to play the snare drum on the backbeats.

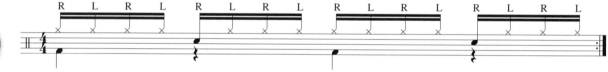

Shuffle Feel

Here is a basic shuffle pattern. As before, you might want to practice various combinations of two and three instruments before you attempt the entire pattern.

Of course, you can also ride on the closed hi-hat and eliminate the hi-hat foot part.

SECTION **3**

Playing, Part 2

CHAPTER 8
MOVING AROUND THE DRUMSET

> **What's Ahead:**
> * Real estate
> * "Around the kit" fills

REAL ESTATE

A drumset covers more real estate than any other instrument. Although pianists and guitar players move their arms a little bit to reach the extremes of the keyboard or fret board, they can do most of their playing just by wiggling their fingers. But because a drumset is so spread out, drummers not only move their arms up and down to make the stroke, they all move their arms back and forth and in practically every direction. The fluid movements made by a good drummer resemble choreography.

Of course, you're not moving like that all the time. Playing grooves on a drumset doesn't involve a lot of movement. Your left hand will likely be positioned over the snare drum and your right hand will probably be over the ride cymbal or hi-hat. You might reach up to crash a cymbal from time to time, but for the most part, your arm movement will be minimal.

But when it's time for a fill or solo, then you have to move your arms and hands quickly around the drumset. You need to be able to get from one tom to another as quickly and smoothly as a guitar player gets from one fret to another or a pianist gets from one key to another—even though frets and keys are only inches apart, whereas some toms can be several feet away from each other.

> If you have a large drumkit, be careful about twisting your body in unusual ways to reach everything, because too much of that can cause injury. The more drums you have, the closer together you should place everything so that you can reach all of your drums and cymbals without straining your muscles. Also remember that having to reach too far to strike something can interfere with your timing.

"AROUND THE KIT" FILLS

Let's start with everyone's favorite, going "around the kit." Start with the snare drum, then move to the small tom, the medium tom, and the floor tom. Then start over. We'll begin with four notes on each drum. (These exercises will all be written for a standard five-piece kit that includes one snare drum and three toms. If you have a larger kit, you can easily adapt these exercises to include more drums.)

R L R L R L R L R L R L R L R L

Don't worry about speed at first—that will come with practice. It is more important that you first develop a smooth flow around the kit. Try not to jerk your arms as you go from drum to drum. Play slowly enough at first so that you can make a flowing motion, without any tension in your arms or hands. If you *feel* tense or stiff, you are going to *sound* tense or stiff.

Notice that starting with the right hand lends itself to moving around the drums in a clockwise direction. Going around the kit like that, no matter how many notes you play on each drum, is a very popular way of playing fills. For some drummers, however, it seems to be the *only* way of playing fills. Yes, it's fun to do, but listeners get tired of the same thing all the time, so put some variety in your playing. For example, let's turn it around by going counter-clockwise. Starting with the left hand will make this easier.

Now try an "X" pattern around the kit, going from snare to medium tom to small tom to floor tom:

Here are some other combinations of the four drums. Experiment with both right-hand and left-hand lead.

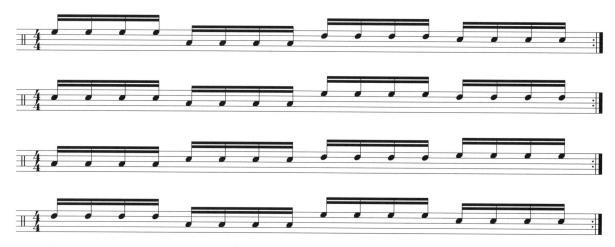

Those are not the only combinations involving each of the drums. Experiment with others to develop your technique as well as your creativity.

Now that you're getting from drum to drum easily, let's add some rhythmic interest. Go back to the previous exercises (along with the ones you created yourself) and replace each group of four sixteenth notes with one of the following patterns. Start with just one pattern for the whole exercise, but once you are comfortable with each pattern, start mixing and matching them.

Even with just four drums and a handful of rhythm patterns, by the time you mix and match all the possible combinations of drums with all the possible combinations of rhythm patterns, you will have a large vocabulary of fill and solo patterns to draw from. But we've still only scratched the surface!

Spend some time playing "threes" (triplets) around the drums. You'll quickly see that instead of leading with a single hand as you go around the kit, you will lead with the opposite hand on each beat. It might feel awkward at first, but you'll quickly get the hang of it and it will do wonders for your control, flexibility, and coordination.

R L R L R L R L R L R L

When you are playing fill and solo patterns, it's often a good idea to have a pulse going on underneath from the bass drum. This not only adds bottom end to the sound, but it also helps you keep the tempo steady, and gives the listeners a reference point. So try playing straight quarter notes on the bass drum while playing various rhythm combinations on the other drums. Here are a couple of examples:

Besides just "going around the kit," you need to be able to mix individual drum sounds together the same way other instrumentalists mix notes on their instruments. Imagine if a guitarist always played each note four times before going to the next note, and yet that is how some drummers play most of their fills. So let's look at some exercises that will help you develop other ways to move around the kit.

Many drummers like to play "melodic" patterns around the toms while filling in on the snare drum. Here are some patterns to help you go from the snare to any tom on any part of the beat:

With the previous patterns, try playing the snare drum notes very softly and the tom notes very loudly. Then come up with your own patterns. The effect should be of a melodic tom solo with background snare drum accompaniment.

CHAPTER 9
FILLS AND SOLOS

What's Ahead:
- Fills
- Solos

Drummers are often told that there are two basic ways to do fills and solos. One way is to play something very difficult and make it look easy. The other way is to play something simple and make it look hard. If you want to impress musicians, go for the first way. If you want a lot of applause from a "general" audience, go for the second way.

Fills and solos are the places where the drummer *finally* gets the spotlight! There is certainly nothing wrong with showing everyone what you can do; after all, you've been backing up the singer and lead guitarist all night while they run around the stage. Sooner or later they are morally obligated to, as James Brown famously said, "Give the drummer some!"

But fills and solos are not just for showing off; there are musical reasons to play them. And however entertaining your fills and solos might be to an audience, the best ones are also musically valid.

FILLS

Okay, so why do we "fill" something? Because it's empty, right? Well, that's why we play drum fills. Good melodies—whether they are being sung with words or played as guitar or keyboard solos—are built from phrases. In between phrases there are short pauses that allow singers (and horn players) to take quick breaths, and also help listeners absorb the material. Think of a phrase as a musical sentence. You've got to have periods and paragraphs so it's not just one big run-on sentence.

Think of your drum fills as the punctuation for those musical sentences. Don't throw in fills in the middle of a phrase. Put them in between the phrases, where the singers and instrumentalists are leaving space. The better you know the song (and the better you are listening), the better you can tailor each fill to fit the appropriate space.

A lot of rock, jazz, blues, country, and other popular song styles are constructed in four- and eight-measure sections. So it's good to develop a feel for four- and eight-bar phrases, as you will often be playing fills at the end of those sections (while the singer takes a quick breath).

Fills do not have to be elaborate. The idea is not to dazzle everyone with your technique every time you play a fill. The idea is just to add a little interest and excitement to the music, while filling a space left by the singer or soloist. Also, remember that the fill should not interrupt the time flow. Think of a fill as just a different way of keeping time for a beat or two.

A fill often leads into a cymbal crash, so we're going to start with the crash as a way of developing a feel for a four-bar phrase. Play the following pattern over and over until playing the crash on the first beat of each four-bar section becomes somewhat automatic, and you don't have to count furiously to keep your place.

Generally, when you play a cymbal crash, it should be supported with a bass drum note.

Now let's add a simple one-beat fill that will lead into the cymbal crash.

Instead of playing all four fill notes on the snare drum, mix them up among the snare and the toms. Here are some possibilities:

Now let's change the fill rhythm each time. We'll stay on the snare drum for the next example, but once you are comfortable with the rhythms, experiment with playing them on different combinations of snare and toms.

In the next example, we are going back to straight sixteenth notes, but we are going to start each fill one sixteenth sooner than the example before it.

Again, once you are comfortable with the rhythms, playing them only on the snare drum, experiment with substituting various tom notes for some (or all) of the snare notes.

Here are a few different rhythm patterns you can substitute for the patterns in the previous example. They are shown just on snare drum, but, of course, you can play them on any combination of drums.

You should be starting to see how much can be done with simple fills covering just a beat or two. And, of course, we have only scratched the surface of rhythmic possibilities.

Chapter 8 has exercises for developing a "vocabulary" for fills and solos. Once you are comfortable with those patterns, you can plug a lot of them into the previous examples for even more fill ideas.

Although most fills just last for a beat or two, they can go on longer—it depends on the song. Also, you won't necessarily play a fill every four bars in every song. In some songs, you might play a fill every eight bars; in a 12-bar blues you might only play fills at the end of the twelfth bar. Again, it depends on the song.

You can also reflect and reinforce the structure of the song by making some fills more important than others. For example, you might just want to play a couple of notes for fills in the middle of phrases, a few more notes for fills at the end of phrases, and your biggest fill of all at the end of the chorus. Likewise, you might want to save your cymbal crashes for the bigger section divisions. Well-placed cymbal crashes can add a lot of excitement to the music, but if you play too many, they can be distracting and interrupt the groove you are trying to create. So save them for when they really count!

SOLOS

Remember what we said earlier about the idea that listeners need space between phrases so they can absorb the material? That applies to drum solos, too. Drummers don't have to play short phrases and take breaks to breathe the way singers and horn players do. We can play non-stop for hours! But we shouldn't do that. That gets *real* boring *real* fast.

Sure, sometimes it is very effective to build up a non-stop intensity that crescendos to a huge climax. But save it for the climax—don't make that the whole solo. Play phrases, just as any musician would. Your audience will get into it much more that way.

One of the challenges with playing phrases, and with playing drum solos in general, is that drummers are usually the only members of the band who have to play a true solo. When guitarists or keyboardists play solos, the rest of the band is accompanying them, so it's easier for them to leave some space. But drummers are often afraid to leave space because then the sound will stop.

There are ways around that, however. Many drummers will maintain a pulse or *ostinato* (short repeated pattern) with a limb or two as a background, while soloing over the pattern with the remaining limbs. Jazz drummer Max Roach kept a simple bass drum/hi-hat pattern going behind his solo drum composition "The Drum Also Waltzes."

On the Beatles *Abbey Road* album, in the song "The End," Ringo Starr kept a steady pulse on the bass drum while playing a series of very melodic phrases on his toms. Let's take a look at it:

The End

Words and Music by
John Lennon and Paul McCartney

Terry Bozzio has a phenomenal ability to keep interesting ostinatos going with his feet while soloing with his hands. Sometimes his ostinatos include both feet and one of his hands, while he plays melodic patterns around his gargantuan kit with his other hand.

You could also ask the rest of the band—or even just a single member—to keep a riff going behind your solo. (After all, you've been playing behind them all night!) Jazz pianist Dave Brubeck kept the basic riff of "Take Five" going behind Joe Morello's legendary solo on the Dave Brubeck Quartet's album *Time Out*. The following are a few measures from the middle section of the solo in which Morello left a lot of space. (The entire solo can be found in the book *Drum Standards*, published by Hal Leonard Corporation.)

Take Five

By Paul Desmond

Even if you don't have someone playing a riff behind your solo, keep in mind that there's actually nothing wrong with brief silences within a drum solo. It gives the listeners a chance to absorb what you just played.

CHAPTER 10
SWING

> **What's ahead:**
> * Swing notation
> * Feel and expression

In its narrowest definition, "swing" is a style of jazz associated with the big band era of the 1930s and '40s. But in a larger sense, "swing" is an elusive quality that generally refers to how the music "feels." If it swings, it is loose, relaxed, and flowing. If it ain't swingin', it's stiff. The term is most often used in regard to jazz, but good rock and funk is sometimes said to swing as well.

SWING NOTATION

In technical terms, "swing" refers to a way of interpreting rhythms to give them a more relaxed feel. For example, let's take straight eighth notes.

When jazz musicians are told to "swing" the eighth notes, they play them like in the next example, transforming the rhythm into a triplet or shuffle-based feel.

Here are several standard rhythm patterns, showing how they would be transformed into swing style:

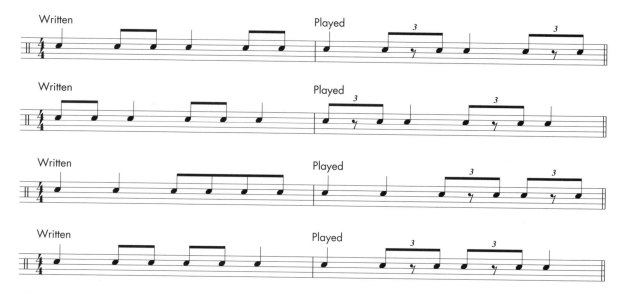

Sometimes, instead of writing jazz or swing rhythms as eighth notes, arrangers and composers will write them as dotted-eighth/sixteenth-note combinations.

But, at most tempos, a jazz musician will still play each pair of notes as if it were the first and third note of a triplet to get that "swing" feel.

How do you know if you are supposed to swing the rhythms? The music might be marked a couple of different ways. At the beginning of the chart, it might simply say "Swing" or "Swing style," telling you to give the rhythms a swing feel. Other times, you might see this: ♫ = ♩♪. In any case, you need to use your ears so you can match the feel the band is getting.

FEEL AND EXPRESSION

We'll take a more in-depth look at jazz timekeeping in Chapter 17. But for now, remember that above everything, swing is a "feel" that sometimes involves playing some notes a tiny bit early or a tiny bit late. Swing also involves expression, which is achieved in a number of ways, but especially by varying the volume of each note so that the music comes out in flowing phrases, much like human speech. Swing also depends on nuance and subtlety, but it starts with the rhythm.

Chapter 17 has a lot of notated examples of jazz rhythms, but if you are not used to hearing jazz, you should start by listening to some jazz records so you can absorb the feel. Trying to learn the jazz feel just from looking at music notation is like trying to learn French from a book without ever having heard anyone speak French.

A great album to start with is *Kind of Blue* by Miles Davis, which is one of the most popular jazz albums ever released. None of the tempos are very fast, and drummer Jimmy Cobb plays very simply, but he swings like crazy! (Or, to borrow an expression from the "swing era," he'll "swing you into bad health.") Put on that album and just tap along on a practice pad so you can hear the music better than you can hear yourself. Try to lock in to the *feel* of the music.

CHAPTER 11

CHAPTER 11
MORE THAN DRUMSTICKS

What's Ahead:
• Brushes
• Mallets
• Alternate sticks

BRUSHES

Brushes are among the most useful—and overlooked—of all the alternative striking devices. Some people think brushes are just for jazz drummers, and they are indeed a vital part of every jazz drummer's arsenal, but they have many other applications as well.

Brushes generally consist of a fan-shaped arrangement of wire strands attached to a handle. Such brushes were developed around 1912 and were often referred to as "flyswatters." Brushes are most often used on the snare drum for timekeeping, but they are sometimes used on cymbals to produce a delicate sound. Brushes can also be used on tom-toms for fills and solos.

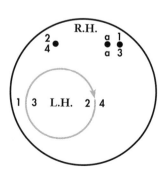

The term *brush* reflects the appearance of the device as well as the way in which it is typically used. Drummers generally slide the left-hand brush over the snare drum head in a rhythmic, circular motion, producing a sustained "swish" sound, while using either a sideswiping motion or direct taps to play rhythmic patterns with the right-hand brush. Brushes are especially popular with jazz drummers, who often use them in ballads to produce a very legato style of timekeeping. But brushes can also be used for fast tempos, as demonstrated by Philly Joe Jones on the Miles Davis recording "Billy Boy," and by drummer Dave Tough who was noted for his ability to power a big band with brushes.

Since brushes are so crucial to jazz, let's talk about their jazz applications first. Again, the basic brush stroke should be a *brushing* movement, in which you slide the brush across the drumhead to get sort of a "swish" sound. This accomplishes a couple of things. First, you may have noticed that when you are playing ride cymbal, the sustain helps fill the sound out. Well, when playing brushes, a jazz player typically keeps the left brush in a steady rotation around the edge of the snare drum head. This is done in rhythm, so it does provide a gentle pulse, but it also fills in the sound in a similar fashion to the ride cymbal. Second, by striking the drum with a sweeping motion of the brush, the sound is thicker and fatter than the staccato sound produced by a drumstick striking the head.

The following diagrams show the movements for some standard jazz brush patterns. In this first pattern, the left-hand brush moves in a circular direction. (Many drummers use a clockwise rotation, but some like to move counter-clockwise. Try both and go with the one that feels most natural to you.) The right hand plays the standard jazz ride pattern (on the snare drum).

Start with the hands at opposite sides of the drumhead: Left hand on the left, right hand on the right. As the left hand sweeps clockwise across the head, the right hand strikes the right side of the drum on beat 1, then crosses over the left hand so as to strike the left side of the drum on beat 2. As this is done, the left hand continues its circle, arriving at its original leftward location on beat 3. Meanwhile, the right hand crosses back to play two strokes (the "a" of beat 2, then beat 3) on the right side. At the stroke of beat 3, the left hand begins a second clockwise rotation. Again, the right hand crosses over, this time to play beat 4 on the left. At the ensuing beat 1, both hands return to their starting positions, and the pattern continues.

At a slow tempo, the left-hand brush might make a full rotation for each beat. At a very fast tempo, it might make a full rotation just once per measure. The idea is to develop a smooth flow. You also want to create a gentle sense of pulse by bearing down on the brush a little bit on the main beats.

At fast tempos, the right-hand brush will most likely tap out the ride rhythm just as if you were using a stick. But the slower the tempo, the more you can "brush" the brush across the head to get a fatter sound. Especially with ballads, these "wider" beats give the other musicians a lot of leeway to shape their phrases and achieve a relaxed feel. The right hand playing may be summarized as follows: "1" on the right side, "2" on the left side, "a3" on the right side, "4" on the left side, the "a1" on the right side, etc.

> In order for brush playing to be effective when you are sliding the brushes over a drumhead, the head must have a textured surface. So if you plan to play a lot of brushes in the traditional way, do not use a clear or smooth snare drum batter head. Use a coated head, and once the coating starts wearing off or losing its texture, replace it.

This next pattern is a favorite for ballads. Let's start with the way you will sometimes see it notated.

The above notation indicates a smooth sound between beats 2 and 3, and beats 4 and 1. The way this is accomplished with brushes is shown in the illustration to the right.

The left-hand brush does its usual rotation. Often, with a ballad, you will make a full rotation on every beat, but, as always, use your ears. If that ends up sounding a little too energetic for a particular ballad, slow it down and just make two rotations per measure.

Drop the right-hand brush on the upper left of the head on beat 2, making a very slight accent, and then sweep it across the head, lifting it up on beat 3. Then repeat the process for beats 4 and 1.

Depending on the song and the sound you want, you might sweep the right-hand brush very evenly, so the volume remains the same between the two beats. You might also give the brush a little "twist" at the end of the stroke so you hear a soft accent on beats 1 and 3. Or, as you sweep the brush across the head, you might slow it down a bit and lighten up on the pressure so that the sound fades out. As always, use your ears. Also, don't just pick one of these methods and use it all the time. Learn all three techniques so all of your ballads don't sound the same.

Drummers will sometimes combine a brush with a stick. For example, country-music drummers will often tap out a ride pattern on the edge of the snare drum with a brush, instead of playing a country-swing ride cymbal pattern. Sometimes they will play backbeats with a regular drumstick while doing that, but often they will use a cross-stick technique with the stick to get a high-pitched "pop" (similar to the sound of Latin claves).

Similarly, jazz drummers will sometimes play a bossa nova by swishing a brush back-and-forth across the snare drum head with the right hand in an eighth-note pattern (imitating the sound of maracas or a shaker), while playing the bossa-nova clave pattern with a cross-stick technique in the left hand. See Chapter 18 on the bossa nova, and Chapter 23 on cross-stick technique.

In acoustic settings, rock drummers will often use brushes instead of sticks to get a softer, warmer, and fatter sound. In the early 1970s, Russ Kunkel started a whole new drumming trend when he played rock-style rhythms with brushes on James Taylor's song "Fire and Rain." Andy Newmark did the same thing on Carly Simon's "Anticipation."

MALLETS

Most mallets fall into one of two categories: mallets designed for timpani and mallets designed for keyboard instruments such as marimba, vibraphone, and xylophone. Mallets designed for marching percussion are usually variations of timpani and/or keyboard mallets.

When playing on drums, timpani mallets give a big, fat sound with a muffled attack. Timpani mallets are the perfect thing when you want to play a dramatic floor-tom roll. It can also be fun to solo with timpani mallets, especially if you turn the snares off so all of your drums sound like toms. The timpani mallets will bring out the lower overtones of the drums.

The heads of most timpani mallets are covered with felt, ranging from very hard and thin for a staccato sound, to very soft and thick for softer playing. For most drumset applications, you will want to go with a medium or "general" pair of timpani mallets, which will give you the best balance between tone and power.

It also sounds great to roll on cymbals with timpani mallets, but if you plan to do a lot of that, you are going to wear out your timpani mallets. If you do a LOT of cymbal rolls, use a pair of medium yarn-wrapped marimba mallets instead. This is what orchestral players use for cymbal rolls. Yarn mallets make a better sound on cymbals and they will hold up much longer.

ALTERNATE STICKS

Several manufacturers offer bundles of dowel rods banded together. These are sold under a variety of names: Hot-Rods (Pro-Mark), Thai Sticks (Calato), Rutes (Vic Firth), Splashstick (Vater), and Mezzo (Zildjian). Most drummers just call them "rods," no matter what the brand. Rods tend to fall somewhere between sticks and brushes, but are closer to sticks in the volume and general tone color they produce. But you can adjust most of them to be tighter or looser around the striking area, and the looser they are set, the fatter the sound they produce.

CHAPTER 12
ADVANCED PLAYING

What's Ahead:
- Drums are easy?!
- Two-bar and four-bar phrases
- Playing the form
- Developing the groove
- Ghost notes
- Mixed meters
- Phrasing over the bar line
- Polyrhythms
- Pushing and pulling

DRUMS ARE EASY?!

Some people are attracted to drumming because they think it's easier than playing other instruments. Granted, there are certain things that other musicians have to deal with that don't affect us. For example, let's say that a band gets a new singer whose voice has a slightly different range than the previous singer. The other instrumentalists might have to relearn all the songs in different keys. The drummer, however, doesn't have to change a thing. And while other instrumentalists have to learn a variety of different notes and chords for each song, drummers can often play the same generic grooves for most of those songs.

But just because drumming *can* be easier in some respects, that doesn't mean that it always *should* be. Good drummers are just as accomplished as any other musicians, and the best drummers don't just play the same generic beats for every song. Even when two songs have the same basic groove and feel, the best drummers find ways to make each drum part unique to the particular song.

In addition, some music is more complex, and playing a simple generic beat just won't cut it. Good drummers must be able to negotiate a variety of time signatures, and sometimes those time signatures can change within a tune, even measure to measure.

We're about to take a look at a few "advanced" drumming concepts that will help take you beyond the basics. But before we do, be aware that "more complex" is not always better. Some musical situations call for a very simple drum part, and if that's what is required, then that is what you need to provide. The key is to believe in what you are playing. If you think a simple beat is "stupid," then you probably won't be putting everything you've got into making it feel great. You have to respect the simplest of beats, be convinced that a simple groove is the absolute perfect thing for a particular song, and then play it with total conviction.

But when it's time to play something more intricate, you have to be ready for that, too—technique-wise as well as attitude-wise.

TWO-BAR AND FOUR-BAR PHRASES

When playing longer phrases, sometimes it is effective to get away from playing a downbeat on the bass drum in every measure. Playing the "1" on the bass drum only every other measure can give the music a better sense of flow.

Two-bar Phrases

The following example shows several different beats and feels, all of which avoid playing the bass drum on beat one in the second measure:

You can apply the same idea to four-bar phrases, only playing a "1" on the bass drum every four bars.

PLAYING THE FORM

The "form" of the tune refers to its structure. Some songs have very simple forms. For example, many blues songs consist of a 12-measure chord structure that is repeated over and over. Many popular songs have what is known as an AABA structure. There is an A section, which is repeated, then a B section (often called the "bridge"), and then the return of the A section. Some songs have two sections, a verse and a chorus, that alternate. And some songs have very complex structures, such as an intro, a first verse, a second verse, a chorus, a transition to a bridge, a solo section, a repeat of the verse and chorus, and an "outro."

There are a wide variety of ways to reflect the form of the tune through your drumming. Here are a few ideas:

- Change the drumbeat slightly for each main section of the music. It probably shouldn't change too much, since it's still the same song. But you might play a simpler version of the beat for the verses and a more complex version during the chorus. Or you might use a one-bar pattern during the verse, and a two-bar pattern during the chorus (in which the first bar is the same one you are using in the verse).

- Change the sound for each section of music. A typical way to do this is by, say, riding on a closed hi-hat during the verses and riding on the ride cymbal during the choruses. You could even ride on the floor tom during a section for a *real* different sound. Jazz drummers often have two different ride cymbals so that they can change the sound behind different soloists.

- Change both the drumbeat and the sound.

- "Announce" the beginning of a new section with a cymbal crash. You might want to lead into the crash with a fill.

DEVELOPING THE GROOVE

Since most songs have sections that repeat, we are often playing the same things over and over. Yes, we want consistency so that, for example, even though verses may differ from choruses in sound, each has its own distinctive character. But there are actually ways to get some variety *within* that overall consistency.

For example, let's say that the following example is going to be your verse pattern, and you are always going to ride on the hi-hat in the verses because you are switching to cymbal for the choruses.

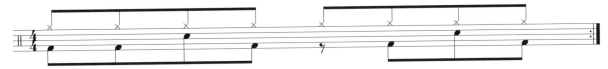

Let's also say that this particular song has three verses. Instead of playing that entire pattern during the first verse, leave out some of it—thin it out by removing a few notes.

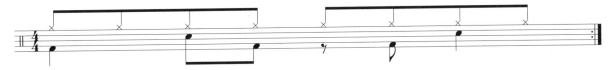

Play the original pattern as written during the second verse, but when you get to the final verse, add some interest and excitement with a few extra notes and sound effects.

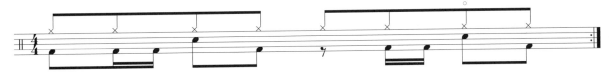

Don't go overboard with this kind of thing, and don't do it in every song, because that in itself will become too predictable. But using that concept occasionally can add to the musicality of your drumming and keep the songs more interesting for the listeners—and for you!

GHOST NOTES

One way to add character to your drumbeats is by using *ghost notes*. These are notes that are played very softly in between the "main" notes. Ghost notes can add interest to a simple beat and also help the feel by creating a more steady flow of notes. Most of the time, ghost notes are played on the snare drum.

In written parts, ghost notes are usually indicated with parentheses, and the "main" notes are indicated with accents to help further distinguish the two types.

MIXED METERS

Not all songs stay in the same time signature throughout. Mixed meters generally fall into two categories: combinations of time signatures that all have the same bottom number (4/4 to 3/4 to

5/4 to 2/4, etc.), and combinations of time signatures that have different lower numbers (4/4 to 5/8 to ₵ to 12/8 to 3/4, etc.).

If the bottom number stays the same, then you just have to concentrate on the number of beats per measure.

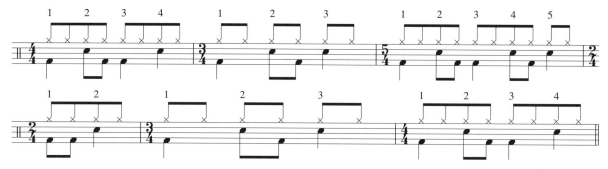

If the bottom number changes, you need to concentrate on a "common denominator" so that you play the transitions smoothly. If you are going from quarter time (2/4, 3/4, 4/4, etc.) to eighth time (3/8, 5/8, 6/8, etc.), then first you need to see if the note values remain consistent, or if the beat remains consistent. If the note values stay consistent, then where the time signature changes you will see something like this: ♪=♪

In the following example, the hi-hat rhythm remains constant, so count all the eighth notes to keep it steady:

Sometimes, however, the beat remains consistent. This usually occurs when going from a time signature such as 4/4 to a time signature such as 12/8 in which three notes are felt as a beat (or the dotted quarter is the beat). In that case, you would see an indication like this: ♩=♩.

In the following example, the bass drum and snare drum maintain a steady pulse, and the cymbal part speeds up in the second measure (like playing triplets in 4/4).

PHRASING OVER THE BAR LINE

You can add interest to a song by superimposing one time signature over another. This is related to polyrhythms, which we will discuss next, but has more to do with phrasing.

If we are phrasing in one time signature (let's say 3/4), while actually playing in another (4/4, say), then the 3/4 phrases will be said to go "over the bar line." For example, look at the following jazz pattern. The ride cymbal is playing a 3/4 pattern while the other instruments maintain a 4/4 feel.

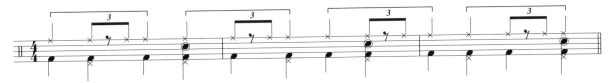

You don't *have* to play two time signatures at once. You might phrase your entire drum part in 3/4 for a few bars, but make sure the rest of the band knows what you're doing! And you might not want to mess around with that kind of phrasing if people are trying to dance.

POLYRHYTHMS

The term *polyrhythms* refers to superimposing different "layers" of rhythm over each other. The previous example of phrasing a cymbal part in 3/4 over a 4/4 groove could be one example of a polyrhythm, but polyrhythms are usually thought of as different divisions of the beat occurring simultaneously.

For example, a popular polyrhythm is "2 against 3." There are various ways to do it, but one way would be to play triplets on the ride cymbal while playing straight eighth notes on the snare drum.

How do you pull something like that off without splitting your brain in half (which would probably be painful)? Here comes math again! We go for the "common denominator." In other words, we subdivide the triplet eighth notes in the cymbal part into triplet sixteenth notes, we subdivide the eighth notes in the snare part to sixteenth-note triplets, and then we see how the two parts align. (The accented notes show the original rhythms.)

If you want to focus on the ride cymbal, then count the resulting "composite rhythm" as shown here:

If you would rather focus on the snare drum part, count this way (using the "1-trip-let & trip-let" counting):

Now let's look at "3 against 4" by putting quarter-note triplets on the snare drum "against" a straight-eighth ride pattern.

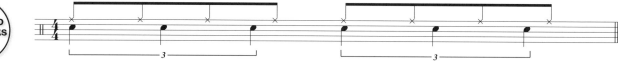

We can arrive at a common denominator of twelve by subdividing each cymbal note into sixteenth-note triplets and each snare note into sixteenths.

You can think of it this way:

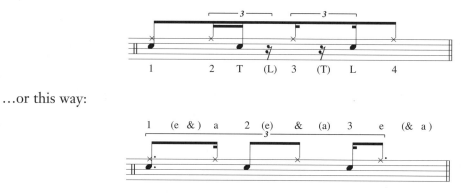

...or this way:

There are endless possibilities for polyrhythms. The secret is to figure out how the hands work together to play a pattern that sounds like two different rhythms when played on two different surfaces.

PUSHING AND PULLING

One of my favorite quotes about rhythm comes from a guitar player rather than a drummer. I was interviewing Rolling Stones guitarist Keith Richards, who was telling me about a producer who wanted the Stones to record with a click track. "Click tracks and metronomes aren't rhythm," Richards said. "That's just timing. Rhythm has to breathe. It has to push and pull. That's why I love playing with Charlie Watts, because he understands that instinctively."

Is Richards saying that it's okay, and even desirable, to rush and drag? No. The overall tempo should stay constant. But within the main pulse, there is room to move around—to let certain notes "lay back," and play others "on top." If absolute metronomic precision made music feel good, then we would have all been put out of work by drum machines in the 1980s. But "perfect" drum machine tracks sound sterile. The timing may be perfect, but there is no feel.

It's the human element that gives music its feel.

CHAPTER 13

CHAPTER 13
DOUBLE-KICK TECHNIQUE AND BEATS

> **What's Ahead:**
> - Double pedal vs. two bass drums
> - Lead with the left or lead with the right?
> - Notation
> - Patterns and grooves

Having two bass drums, or a double bass pedal, can add a lot of power to your playing and enable you to play patterns that you would never be able to pull off with just one foot.

DOUBLE PEDAL VS. TWO BASS DRUMS

Some drummers prefer two bass drums to a double pedal because they feel that the sound is much bigger when they are playing fast patterns between the two drums, and each one gets that little bit of extra time to ring before the next stroke.

Others prefer double pedals because they feel that it's easier to get a consistent sound on one drum, and more difficult to try to get two drums tuned exactly the same. (Some double kick players tune their two bass drums differently to get a wider range of sounds, but most tune them the same.) A double pedal is also easier to carry around and fit on a stage than another bass drum—though you can't mount toms on it!

Even if you prefer two bass drums, you might also want to have a double pedal for situations in which you cannot fit another drum on a small stage.

When playing two bass drums or a double pedal, clamp the top hi-hat cymbal down on the bottom cymbal so that you can ride on a closed hi-hat without having to hold the hi-hat pedal down with your foot.

LEAD WITH THE LEFT OR LEAD WITH THE RIGHT?

The double kick (or pedal) players I've known have been divided pretty equally into two camps: Those who play the "main" beats with the right foot and the "in between" beats with the left, and those who do the opposite. I also know a couple of players who have made an effort to learn every possible pattern leading with either foot so that they have maximum flexibility. It doesn't matter which method you use as long as it works for you and sounds good.

NOTATION

Generally, the bass drum played by the right foot is notated on the bottom space of the staff, where a single bass drum would be notated. The "secondary" bass drum is notated below that on the bottom line.

PATTERNS AND GROOVES

Many players use double bass drums to keep a steady pulse, almost like a ride cymbal. Here are some basic patterns to master. These are all notated as "right foot lead," but experiment with reversing each pattern and ultimately use whichever feels best to you and gives you the most control.

Here are a few more basic grooves using double bass drum:

CHAPTER 14
LATIN AND WORLD PERCUSSION

What's Ahead:
- Timbales
- Cowbell
- Agogos
- Bongos
- Woodblock
- Pedal-operated instruments
- Shakers and Maracas
- Tambourines

A variety of Latin and "world" percussion instruments can be incorporated into drumset playing to add color. In many cases, they can be mounted around the kit and played with drumsticks, but others are best played with a bare hand or two. We'll look at a few of the most popular.

TIMBALES

Timbales are single-headed drums with metal shells that look and sound very much like tom-toms, but with a brighter sound. In fact, drummers who play in bands that specialize in Latin music often have timbales mounted on their bass drums instead of traditional toms. Other drummers sometimes mount them off to the side of their setups.

COWBELL

A cowbell is probably the Latin instrument most likely to be found on a drumset. Many hard rock drummers like to use them for quarter-note rides during songs. And, of course, they add a nice color to Latin tunes.

There are many sizes available. The big ones have a rich, dark sound, and the small ones cut through a loud band better. You can get various types of mounting brackets so that you can mount a cowbell practically anywhere on the kit. If the cowbell you buy sounds a little too "clangy" and you want a drier sound, try wrapping some black electrical tape around it.

AGOGOS

Agogo bells are part of the cowbell family. They usually come in pairs, one high pitched and one medium or low pitched. There are two general types. Brazilian agogos are cone-shaped and usually have a sleeker appearance. African agogos are rougher looking and the mouths of the bells are usually more oval than round.

Brazilian agogos   African agogos

BONGOS

Bongos are traditionally played with the hands, so they don't turn up on drumsets very often, but they can add an interesting color to your kit, and because they are so small, it's easy to fit them in. If you plan to hit them with sticks, be sure to have synthetic heads rather than skin heads on them.

WOODBLOCK

Woodblocks, and their modern counterpart the JamBlock, are about the same size as a medium cowbell and can easily be mounted within a drumkit. Woodblocks produce a high-

pitched sound that really cuts through. Some drummers like to ride on them when playing a quarter-note feel. Other drummers like to use them to get a clave-like sound, rather than using a cross-stick technique on a snare drum.

Jam Block

Woodblock

PEDAL-OPERATED INSTRUMENTS

In recent years, manufacturers (notably Latin Percussion, or LP) have come out with mounting brackets that allow you to play instruments such as cowbells or JamBlocks with a bass drum pedal. It has become popular for some drummers to play the Latin *clave* pattern with the left foot on a pedal-operated JamBlock or cowbell, leaving the hands free for other patterns and rhythms.

SHAKERS AND MARACAS

The next time you play a soft ballad or bossa nova, instead of riding eighth notes on a cymbal or hi-hat, put down your right stick and pick up a shaker or maraca and keep your eighth notes going that way. You'll need to practice coordinating the back-and-forth motion with your other limbs, but you'll catch on very quickly, and substituting a shaker for a ride cymbal or hi-hat can really spice up a tune.

Shaker

Maracas

TAMBOURINES

There are many tambourines manufactured today that are designed to be mounted as part of a drumset. Many drummers mount them just over their hi-hat so they can ride on the tambourine, or play something back and forth between the tambourine and hi-hat.

There are also tambourine jingles that can be mounted to the top of a hi-hat, so that whenever you bring the hi-hat cymbals together with the pedal, you also get a tambourine sound.

audio tracks 30

Track 30 contains audio examples of the following instruments discussed in this chapter, in the following order: timbales, cowbell, agogo bells, bongos, woodblock, shaker and tambourine.

SECTION **4**

Styles

CHAPTER 15
EARLY ROCK 'N' ROLL

What's Ahead:
- Shuffle beats
- Straight beats
- The Bo Diddley beat

Early rock 'n' roll was a mixture of jazz, blues, and country music, and most of the early rock drummers had started out playing one or more of those styles. Therefore, early rock 'n' roll songs often had beats and feels borrowed from other styles of music.

On early rock 'n' roll recordings, the snare drum, bass drum, and ride cymbal (or hi-hat) were all played at about the same volume. But as rock music evolved (and as guitar players got bigger amplifiers), rock drummers began hitting the snare drum and bass drum a *lot* harder, keeping the ride cymbal or hi-hat patterns very much in the background. So if you want to make it sound more like early rock 'n' roll, lighten up on the bass drum and the snare drum backbeats, and put more emphasis on your ride cymbal or hi-hat.

SHUFFLE BEATS

Reflecting the jazz, blues, and country influence, many early rock songs were built on the shuffle rhythm. Here is a very basic version:

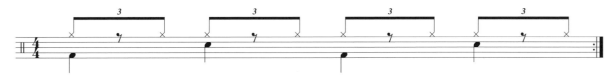

Here's a "jazzy" version of the shuffle that appeared on some of the early rock 'n' roll records. The quarter-note pulse is emphasized more than the snare-drum backbeats.

Even when piano players such as Little Richard and guitar players such as Chuck Berry were playing straight eighth notes, the drummers often had just a hint of a shuffle (or swing) in their playing, creating a rhythmic tension that gave early rock 'n' roll its distinctive feel.

STRAIGHT BEATS

One of the simplest rock 'n' roll beats is also one of the most widely used. It's the beat on Roy Orbison's hit "Oh, Pretty Woman," and has also been used on countless Motown recordings as well as hit records by such artists as the Rolling Stones, Jefferson Airplane, and Young Rascals.

Oh, Pretty Woman

Words and Music by
Roy Orbison and Bill Dees

Ringo Starr gave that beat a unique sound on the verses of "Come Together" by the Beatles by playing the eighth-note ride on the floor tom with straight quarters on small tom and bass drum. The combination of the toms and the slow tempo gave the drumming an ominous sound.

Come Together

Words and Music by
John Lennon and Paul McCartney

Here is one of the most popular early rock 'n' roll beats, which has been used on hundreds of songs. It is sometimes referred to as the "Twist" beat, referring to a dance fad of the early 1960s, but this beat was used long before the Twist became popular, and continued to be used well into the 1960s. Ringo Starr used this beat on several Beatles' songs, such as "Please Please Me."

Please Please Me

Words and Music by
John Lennon and Paul McCartney

Some drummers give this beat a slightly syncopated feel by accenting the second snare drum note.

There are many variations of this beat, which have been used on numerous recordings. Here are a few:

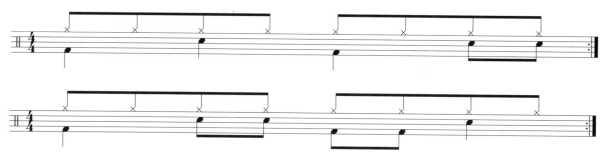

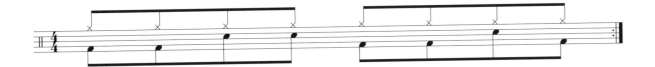

Instead of playing snare drum on the two eighth notes in the above patterns, play a tom-tom. You can also play the eighth-note ride pattern on a floor tom instead of on ride cymbal or hi-hat. Quite a few hit records have featured that very beat!

THE BO DIDDLEY BEAT

One of the most important rock 'n' roll innovators of the 1950s was a guitarist/singer/composer named Bo Diddley. Many of his songs featured a beat that was based on the Latin clave pattern.

Diddley's drummer would often play slightly shuffled eighth notes on the floor tom, accenting the notes of the clave pattern, and reinforcing those accents with the bass drum.

Here is a variation of the Bo Diddley beat using the full kit:

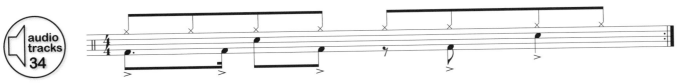

Bo Diddley always had a maraca player who played straight eighths (with a hint of a shuffle feel) along with the drummer. So if you want to get the real Bo Diddley sound, you might try shaking a pair of maracas with your right hand while playing the variation shown above.

Photo courtesy of Photofest, Inc.

Bo Diddley

CHAPTER 16
BLUES

> **What's Ahead:**
> * Blues shuffle

BLUES SHUFFLE

Besides being a style in its own right, the blues forms the basis of many jazz, rock, folk, gospel, and even country tunes. Blues can be played with just about any rhythm feel, but it is most identified with the shuffle.

Basic Shuffle Patterns

The shuffle can be notated with a triplet pattern in 4/4 time, as shown at the beginning of Chapter 15. But it is often notated in 12/8 time, as shown here.

Many blues drummers play the shuffle rhythm with both hands, while keeping a straight pulse on the bass drum and playing backbeats with the hi-hat pedal.

There are many variations of the shuffle. Here are a couple:

If a guitar player is strumming the basic shuffle pattern, the drummer can play more "open," establishing the shuffle feel without playing every note. Here is just one example:

If the blues tempo is a little slower, many drummers play continuous eighths (the same as playing straight triplets in 4/4).

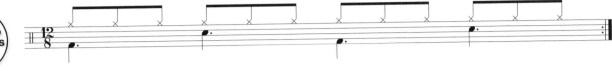

At slower tempos, some drummers like to combine continuous eighths on the ride cymbal (or hi-hat) with the shuffle rhythm on bass drum and snare drum.

For *very* slow blues, drummers often divide the second note of the first and third three-note eighth ride pattern into sixteenths, giving them this:

For the half-time shuffle feel, the ride pattern stays the same, but the backbeat is placed on beat three.

For an extremely fast shuffle, you can alternate hands between the closed hi-hat and snare drum. If you want to retain a more traditional drumset sound, you can do it this way:

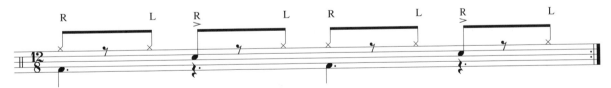

Some drummers just play the whole thing on the snare drum, sometimes with brushes instead of sticks.

On the B.B. King classic "The Thrill Is Gone," drummer Herbie Lovelle created a feel with a lot of forward momentum during the first two choruses by playing the snare drum on every beat—the first three beats very softly, and beat 4 with a heavy accent—and only playing bass drum in the middle of the bar.

The Thrill Is Gone

Words and Music by
Roy Hawkins and Rick Darnell

On the slow blues "Third Degree" on Eric Clapton's *From the Cradle* album, drummer Jim Keltner created a smooth, snaky groove with brushes by playing the standard jazz ride pattern with the right hand, while swishing the left-hand brush across the head. (Review the description of this technique in Chapter 11.)

Third Degree

Written by
Willie Dixon and Eddie Boyd

On "Blues Leave Me Alone," also from Clapton's *From the Cradle*, Keltner gave a lilt to the groove by accenting the upbeats of the shuffle pattern in the hi-hat, and also frequently played all three eighth notes of the final beat.

Blues Leave Me Alone

Written by
James A. Lane

In addition to the types of patterns shown here, blues beats may be applied to a variety of rock, jazz, and funk patterns. Most blues musicians will tell you, "It ain't *what* you play, it's *how* you play it."

CHAPTER 17

JAZZ

> **What's Ahead:**
> - Swing ride
> - The role of the bass drum
> - Independence
> - Time, feel, and rhythm
> - Other time signatures
> - Soloing and trading fours
> - Fusion

More than any other type of music, jazz is about the self-expression of the musicians who play it. Although they often play tunes written by other composers, the main purpose of those tunes is to provide a framework for improvised solos. And they never play the same solo twice.

Even when the musicians are playing the "head" of the tune, which is the part the composer wrote, jazz players typically experiment with different ways to play it. They might play it faster or slower than the original, change the feel from swing to Latin, or even change the time signature.

Jazz drummers, therefore, do not tend to play a specific, repetitive rhythmic pattern throughout a tune. Rather, they concentrate on pulse, forward momentum, and swing, letting the feeling of the moment—as well as what the other band members are playing—influence what they play at a given time.

SWING RIDE

The emphasis is generally on the ride cymbal, which is the primary timekeeping element. The pedalled hi-hat usually contributes a soft backbeat. The snare drum often plays freely, reinforcing important accents. The bass drum will sometimes maintain a very soft pulse, while other times it will combine with the snare drum to reinforce accents or create counter-rhythms.

The traditional ride cymbal pattern is played with a triplet feel, notated like this:

This pattern is also sometimes notated like this:

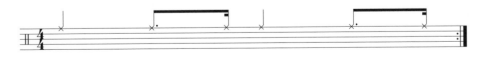

or like this:

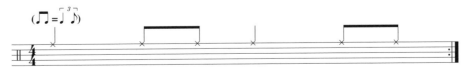

But it should always be played with the triplet feel.

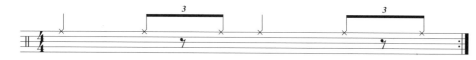

There are different ways to approach the ride cymbal feel. Often beats 2 and 4 are accented slightly.

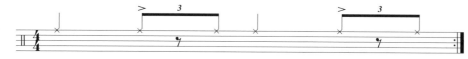

In some cases, you will want to emphasize the quarter notes, and play the "swung" notes very lightly.

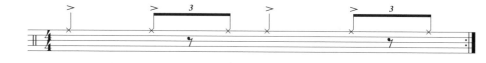

Elvin Jones gave his ride cymbal playing a very personal identity by accenting the "swung" notes.

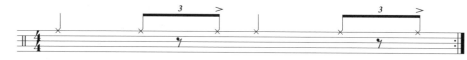

Sometimes the traditional ride pattern is played on the hi-hat. The foot continues playing beats 2 and 4 on the hi-hat pedal, so the notes on beats 1 and 3 are open, the notes on 2 and 4 are closed, and the "swung" notes are generally half open.

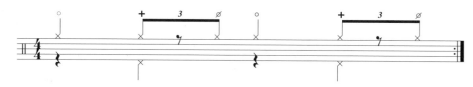

THE ROLE OF THE BASS DRUM

In the early days of jazz (the Dixieland and Ragtime eras) up through the Swing era or Big Band era, jazz drummers usually played straight quarter notes pretty loudly on the bass drum to help hold the large bands together.

As bebop developed in the 1940s, and small combos began to replace big bands, drummers did not have to play the bass drum as loudly to hold the bands together. The ride cymbal and hi-hat became the most important timekeepers, and the snare drum and bass drum were used for accents and counter-rhythms. When bop drummers played occasional loud accents on the bass drum, it was referred to as "dropping bombs."

Some people think that bop drummers only used the bass drum for those occasional accents. But according to bebop drumming pioneer Max Roach, that is not true. "We played the bass drum, but [on recordings] there were never any microphones near our feet; they would have one mic above the drumset and that was all. It was funny to me that when I would hear a recording, I didn't hear the bass drum, because in those days the bass drum was always prevalent."

Some drummers refer to the technique of playing very soft quarter notes on the bass drum as "feathering" the drum. That was easier to do in the 1940s and '50s because drummers used lamb's wool bass drum beaters that were larger and softer than today's hard felt beaters. Thus many modern jazz drummers have abandoned keeping a "straight four" on the bass drum. But when you are first learning jazz rhythms, playing quarters softly on the bass drum can help you feel the pulse and lock in with the bass player.

INDEPENDENCE

Jazz drummers often use the word "independence" to refer to the ability to maintain the ride cymbal pattern while playing counter-rhythms with the snare drum and/or bass drum.

Here are some basic patterns that will help you begin to develop such independence on the snare drum. Play the bass drum very softly while practicing these patterns. (On the accompanying CD track, each measure is played two times.)

Here are some independence patterns using both snare drum and bass drum. (Again, each pattern is played twice.)

Comping

The various accents that jazz drummers play on the snare drum and bass drum when backing a soloist are often referred to as "comping" patterns. The word "comp" comes from the word "accompany," and it is the same thing that pianists and guitarists do when playing behind a soloist. They are providing just enough harmony to support the soloist's melodic explorations. The drummer is providing rhythmic stimulation.

Jazz vibraphonist Gary Burton compares comping to the little comments you might make when someone is explaining something to you or telling you a story. You might say things like, "I see," "Oh, really," "Wow!," or "Tell me more," just to let the person know you are following what he is saying, and to encourage him to keep going.

That's how your snare/bass drum comping should work behind soloists. Remember, the idea is to *accompany* them, not to compete or steal the spotlight. Listen carefully to soloists and try to reinforce the mood they are creating. As they build in intensity, you should increase the intensity of what you are playing. If they are playing slowly and lyrically, you should offer gentle accompaniment.

Although you always want to accompany, that's not to say that you can't stimulate, encourage, or inspire the soloist by kicking the energy up a notch if the tune seems to be dragging.

TIME, FEEL, AND RHYTHM

Anticipated Beats

In jazz tunes, musicians will sometimes add some extra syncopation to a tune by "anticipating" a beat—playing it early. For example, instead of hitting a new chord on the first beat of a measure, they will hit it on the "and of four" of the previous measure. Or instead of changing chords on the third beat of a measure, they will change the chord on the "and" of the second beat. These are called anticipated beats or "push" beats.

Here is how a jazz drummer might reinforce on "anticipated" chord played on the "and" of the fourth beat:

Here is the way you might anticipate the third beat:

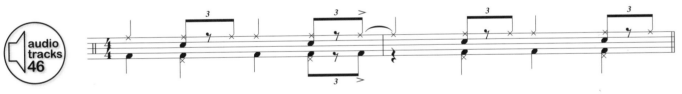

Anticipations can occur on any beat, and you can have two or more in a row, creating a particularly syncopated feel.

> Some songs are so filled with anticipated beats that if you reinforce all of them with the cymbal and bass drum, the time feel will become very choppy. In such cases, it's often best for the drummer to play straight time through most of the tune, just hitting occasional anticipated beats. By playing straight time, you will be providing a good reference point for the other musicians (and the listeners) so that they don't lose the basic pulse amid all of those push beats.

Breaking Up the Time

During the Bebop era, which began in the 1940s, drummers started "breaking up" the time on the ride cymbal, getting away from the repetitive traditional jazz ride pattern that was used during the Swing era. The emphasis was placed on the quarter-note pulse, and "swung" notes were scattered around almost at random.

Here is an example of how a jazz drummer might break up the time on the ride cymbal during an eight-measure section of a tune:

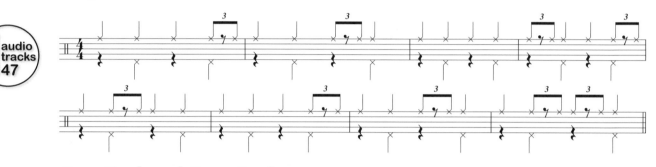

Two Feel and Four Feel

Some jazz tunes are felt "in two," and some are felt "in four." Many jazz tunes use both feels. When a tune is played "in two," the emphasis is on beats one and three, and the bass player will most likely be playing on just those two beats. The drummer should do likewise, and also emphasize the backbeats.

When playing "in four," the emphasis is on the quarter-note pulse. The bass player will be playing a "walking" bass pattern, consisting primarily of quarter notes (but will often throw in some "swung" notes here and there). The drummer should even out the ride cymbal so that the 2 and 4 are not accented, and lock in the quarter notes with the bass player. Drummers will often leave out one of the "swung" notes from the cymbal pattern and use a cross-stick on the snare drum on beat four.

Many standard jazz tunes (called, appropriately enough, "standards") are 32 measures long and are divided into four eight-measure groups in an AABA structure. The first two A sections will often be played with a "two" feel, the B section (called the "bridge") will be played with a "four" feel, and the final A section will return to a "two" feel. This 32-bar section is called the "head" of the tune.

In big band settings, drummers sometimes play the "two" feel of the A sections by riding on the hi-hat, then switch to the ride cymbal for the "four" feel of the B section, and go back to the hi-hat for the final A section.

After the head is played (sometimes twice), the chord pattern continues while individual musicians take improvised solos. Often, the entire solo section is played "in four." After the solos, the head is played one more time, with the A sections played "in two" and the B section played "in four."

Generally, the drummer will play fairly steady, repetitive patterns during the head, then start breaking up the time while accompanying the solos.

Because jazz drummers play so much on the ride cymbal, many jazz drummers use two or even three different ride cymbals so that they can change the sound behind each soloist.

Double-time and Half-time Feels

Sometimes, to add a bit of excitement to a tune, the rhythm section will go into a "double-time" feel. One way to do this is simply to play everything twice as fast as the original tempo.

Another approach is to double-time only the ride pattern, but keep the pulse and backbeats in the original tempo.

The opposite approach—the "half-time" feel—would be to keep the ride pattern in the original tempo and move the backbeat to beat three.

OTHER TIME SIGNATURES

Jazz Waltz

Jazz makes more use of the 3/4 time signature than styles such as rock, blues, and funk. There are several ways to play a jazz waltz. Here are a few:

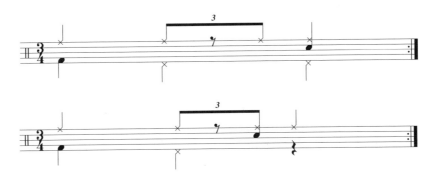

Odd Time

Whereas most swing and bebop tunes were in 4/4 or 3/4, modern jazz musicians often like to explore other time signatures. A pioneer in making odd times swing was Joe Morello with the Dave Brubeck Quartet. Their most famous recording was "Take Five," which was in 5/4 and featured an extended drum solo over a piano vamp.

Tunes in 5/4 generally have either a 2-3 structure, meaning that the primary downbeats are beats 1 and 3 (like a 2/4 measure connected to a 3/4 measure) or 3-2, with the primary downbeats being on 1 and 4 (like a 3/4 measure followed by a 2/4 measure).

Here are a couple of ways you might play 5/4 that is structured 2-3:

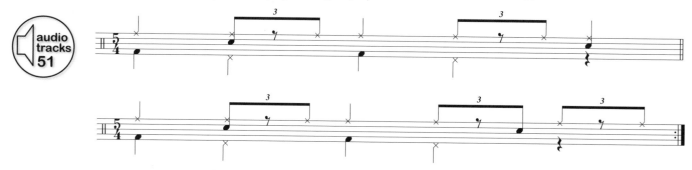

For the 3-2 structure, you can just flip the above patterns, using the pattern for the last three beats as the first three beats, and the first two as the last two.

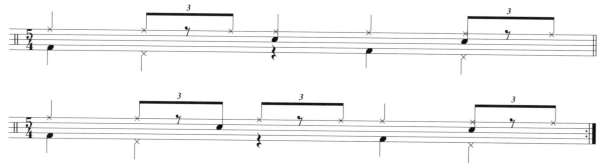

There are certainly other ways to play 5/4 jazz, but those will get you started.

Jazz in 7/4 can be subdivided several ways, such as 2-2-3, 2-3-2, or 3-2-2. Here are some typical timekeeping patterns:

SOLOING AND TRADING FOURS

In jazz, drum solos usually take up specific amounts of time, determined by the length of the "head." A "chorus" is equivalent to one time through the changes, so a chorus of many standard jazz tunes will be 32 measures, while the chorus of a blues-based jazz tune might be 12 measures.

Often, the drummer will be given just a single chorus in which to play a solo. When the other musicians are playing their solos, the rhythm section (piano, bass, drums, guitar) keeps playing behind them, providing chord changes and rhythm. So it's pretty easy for them to know when they've reached the end of a chorus.

But when drummers solo, the rest of the band usually stops, so you have to know where you are at all times. For this reason, it is good to develop a feel for four-bar and eight-bar phrases. That will help you keep your place, and it will generally make your solos more musical.

Of course, even if you are counting meticulously, if you are being very creative rhythmically, the other musicians might not be able to follow you. In a *Modern Drummer* magazine interview, Elvin Jones once commented on playing with musicians who couldn't follow a drum solo. "I had to have a 'device' to bring them back in," Jones said. "That device was a long roll and a vigorous nodding of the head."

When practicing solo patterns, try to keep the hi-hat going on beats 2 and 4. That will provide a reference point for you and the other musicians, which will allow you to be more rhythmically creative with your soloing without losing the basic pulse.

Sometimes, instead of giving the drummer a complete chorus, the drummer will be asked to "trade fours" with one or more of the other players. This means that one player will solo for four measures (with full band accompaniment), and then the drummer will solo for four measures (generally with no accompaniment). This is where it is especially important to develop a feel for a four-bar phrase.

In the best situations, "trading fours" becomes a musical conversation, with the players listening to each other and picking up on each others' melodic and rhythmic ideas so that the music has a flow. In the worst examples, when the drummer solos, it's as though the music screeches to a halt while the drummer shows off his or her "chops," and then the tune starts up again.

After trading fours, some groups like to build to a climax by trading "twos" and sometimes even "ones" before returning to the "head."

It is often said that jazz is played from the top down and rock is played from the bottom up. In other words, with jazz drumming the primary rhythmic drive comes from the ride cymbal and hi-hat. With rock, the main thrust comes from the bass drum and snare drum.

FUSION

Original Pat Metheny Group drummer Danny Gottlieb once described a "fusion beat" as: "a beat that has parts of a jazz groove and parts of a rock beat, but doesn't sound like either one."

"Fusion" is a term coined in the early 1970s to refer to a blend of jazz and rock. Early fusion—pioneered by such drummers as Tony Williams, playing with both Miles Davis and Herbie

Hancock; Jack DeJohnette, also with Davis; Airto Moreira with Chick Corea; Andy Newmark with Sly and the Family Stone; and Bob Moses with Gary Burton—was more jazz-like. There was an emphasis on pulse over beat, and the ride cymbal would break up time in a jazz fashion, but with a straight-eighth feel rather than a swing feel. The snare and bass drums were typically used lightly to reinforce accents rather than to keep a specific "beat." The hi-hat pedal was often played on all four beats to emphasize the pulse (an innovation generally credited to Tony Williams).

Here is an eight-measure groove in the style of early fusion.

Gradually fusion became increasingly rock-like, with more emphasis on bass drum and snare drum, but the jazz element was retained through the constant variations that drummers played. A lot of the "fusion" played in the 1980s and '90s had a strong funk influence.

CHAPTER 18
LATIN

What's Ahead:
- Afro-Cuban
- Brazilian
- Other Latin Rhythms

The term "Latin" is often used generically to refer to styles from Cuba, Puerto Rico, the Caribbean, Spain, Mexico, and South America. Some people think of Brazilian patterns as "Latin," but Brazilian music is more jazz-like than most other "Latin" music, so we will look at it separately.

AFRO-CUBAN

Cuban and Puerto Rican rhythms are often referred to as "Afro-Cuban," reflecting the African origins of the music. Afro-Cuban rhythms have strict parts played (in their purest form) by congas, bongos, timbales, cowbells, and claves (thick wooden sticks that are struck against each other to produce a high-pitched, penetrating sound). The rhythm played by the claves is, in fact, called the *clave*, and it is the fundamental pattern that forms the basis of most Afro-Cuban rhythms. It appears in two distinct versions:

3-2 clave

2-3 clave

Drummer Horatio "El Negro" Hernandez has developed the ability to keep the clave pattern with his left foot on a woodblock mounted to a pedal, while he plays various patterns or solos with his remaining limbs.

In an Afro-Cuban percussion section, each instrument stays with a very specific pattern, unless it is that player's time to solo. So when playing drumset versions of Afro-Cuban rhythms, the drummer should not play a lot of variations. The idea is to set up a very strong groove.

On drumset, the sound of the claves is often imitated with a cross-stick technique on the snare drum. The tom-toms and bass drums imitate the sounds of bongos, congas, and timbales, and snares are often turned off so that the snare drum has a tom-like sound. Drummers who play a lot of Afro-Cuban beats often have a cowbell mounted on their kit, which they use instead of riding on a cymbal or the hi-hat. The bell of a cymbal can also be used to imitate the cowbell sound.

The following are some popular Afro-Cuban grooves. Many of these are more "dance band" versions than "authentic" rhythms, as genuine Afro-Cuban percussion sections rarely use drumsets.

Cha-Cha-Cha

Play the cymbal part on the bell, or substitute a cowbell. After playing the cross-stick snare drum note on beat 2, just reach up with the back end of the stick for the two tom notes on beat 4.

Rumba

This is a very popular cymbal pattern for Latin rhythms. The cross-stick plays a variation of the clave pattern.

Mambo

This is very similar to the rumba. The differences in the bass drum parts are crucial.

New York Mozambique

This is a blend of Cuban Carnival music and funk.

Songo

This is a Cuban feel with some funk-like syncopation.

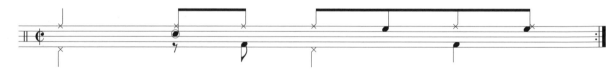

Nanigo

Many Cuban grooves are notated in 6/8, such as this popular rhythm.

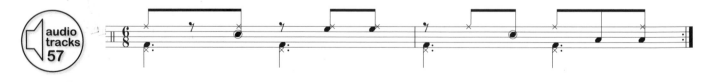

Mozambique

Here is a more traditional version of the Mozambique.

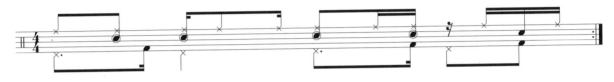

Salsa

"Salsa" is a generic version of Cuban music. This is good when you want something that sounds "Latin-y," but that doesn't require an authentic rhythm.

BRAZILIAN

Brazilian music is very jazz-like. Although each rhythm has its own specific pattern, players tend to throw in a lot of variations and concern themselves more with the "feel" of a rhythm than with the specific pattern. For that reason, Brazilian rhythms are often incorporated into jazz.

Samba

This is the most important Brazilian rhythm of all. It is the centerpiece of the Brazilian Carnaval parade, a celebration equivalent to Mardi Gras in New Orleans.

Samba is played with great spirit, and in a "two" feel. The bass drum part reproduces the pattern played on the Brazilian surdo, which looks like a huge floor tom. Note the accent in the bass drum on the second beat. This is an important element of the samba feel.

There are many different ways to play samba on drumset. Here are just a few:

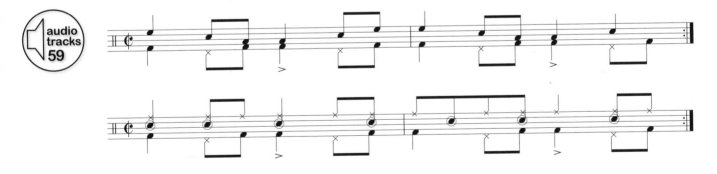

When playing samba with straight eighths on the ride, be sure to keep it loose.

Here's a jazz samba that Peter Erskine likes to use, from his book *The Drum Perspective* (Hal Leonard Corporation):

Bossa Nova

The great Brazilian percussionist Airto Moreira says that the bossa nova started out as "apartment music." In other words, people who lived in apartments had to find a softer way of playing that would not bother the neighbors. So, the bossa nova emerged as a "gentle" way to play a samba.

The bass drum pattern is very samba-like. The eighth-note ride is played by Brazilians on shakers, but most drumset players use hi-hat or ride cymbal. Some drummers imitate the shaker sound by swishing a brush across the snare drum head in steady eighth notes. The snare drum is played with a cross-stick technique (see Chapter 23), using a pattern resembling the Afro-Cuban clave rhythm.

Batucada

A Batucada is a jam played by percussion only. It basically has a samba feel. The eighth notes should be played with a loose feel, almost swing-like.

OTHER LATIN RHYTHMS

Beguine

This rhythm is popular in dance bands.

Tango

Another popular dance-band rhythm is the Tango, from Argentina. Play this on the small tom or on the snare drum with the snares turned off.

Bolero

Reggae

The reggae style comes from Jamaica. As with many Latin styles, it is very much about feel, so you need to listen to reggae music to pick up the groove. For the "real thing," check out masters like Bob Marley, Peter Tosh, and Burning Spear. Such artists as Eric Clapton, the Police, and the Rolling Stones have incorporated reggae "riddims" into their music.

One of the most typical reggae rhythms is called the one-drop, in which the bass drum strikes on beat 3. (In some respects, it is similar to the strong "2" beat in samba.) Here is a basic version:

Reggae is also often played with a shuffle feel, so try the previous pattern by playing the straight-eighth notes with a shuffle feel. Here is a variation of that pattern that can also be played straight or with a shuffle feel. (CD Track 66 is played with the shuffle feel.)

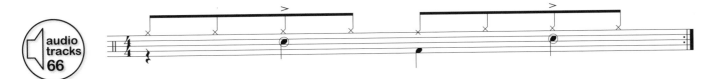

Here's how Stewart Copeland used a reggae feel for the Police hit "Don't Stand So Close to Me."

Don't Stand So Close to Me

Music and Lyrics by
Sting

A reggae influence is also obvious on Copeland's groove to another Police hit, "Roxanne."

Roxanne

Music and Lyrics by
Sting

Photo by Ebet Roberts/Redferns Music Picture Library

Stewart Copeland

CHAPTER 19
ROCK

> **What's Ahead:**
> - Quarter-note ride
> - Eighth-note ride
> - Sixteenth-note ride

We already looked at early rock beats in Chapter 15. Now we'll look at some of the patterns that drummers have used as rock has developed over the past half-century. We will group the beats according to ride pattern.

QUARTER-NOTE RIDE

Drummers use quarter-note ride patterns for different reasons. Sometimes, it simply has to do with the tempo of the song. If the tempo is really fast, anything busier than quarter notes might make the music sound cluttered.

In many cases, a quarter-note ride pattern is used for power. Just as guitar players use "power chords" that only contain a couple of notes, hard rock and metal drummers often play "power beats" that are about as basic as you can get. But when played with drive (and a healthy dose of attitude), such patterns can really get people up on their feet.

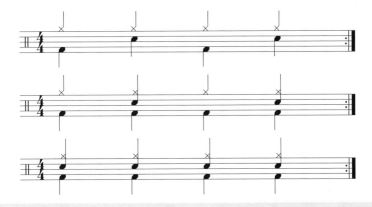

On the basic quarter-note beats, experiment with different sounds in addition to the closed hi-hat sound. For example, open the hi-hat slightly to get a "sloshy" sound, use the bell of the ride cymbal, use a mounted cowbell or woodblock, or use a floor tom.

Drummers will often add offbeat eighth notes on the bass drum to quarter-note grooves, as Tico Torres did on Bon Jovi's "Born to Be My Baby."

Born to Be My Baby

Words and Music by Jon Bon Jovi,
Richie Sambora and Desmond Child

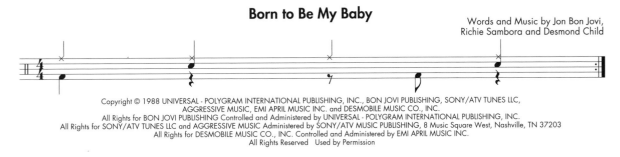

Here are some variations of that type of feel:

A quarter-note ride does not always translate to a quarter-note feel. The drummer might keep quarter notes on the ride cymbal or hi-hat just to keep from cluttering up the band's sound, but be creating an eighth-note, shuffle, or sixteenth-note feel with the snare drum and bass drum parts.

Here are some typical eighth-note feels with a quarter-note ride pattern:

Jimmy Chamberlin set up this strong eighth-note groove on the snare and bass with quarter notes on the ride cymbal on the Smashing Pumpkins' song "Zero" from the album *Mellon Collie and the Infinite Sadness.*

Zero

Words and Music by
Billy Corgan

On "Mississippi Queen" by Mountain, drummer Corky Laing set up a half-time feel by putting the snare drum on beat 3. (Note the cymbal crash that replaces the hi-hat note on beat 3 of the second measure.)

Mississippi Queen

Words and Music by Leslie West,
Felix Pappalardi, Corky Laing and David Rea

Here are some shuffle feels with a quarter-note ride:

Peter Criss used a shuffle feel with a quarter-note ride in the Kiss song "Detroit Rock City."

Detroit Rock City

Words and Music by
Paul Stanley and Bob Ezrin

Photo courtesy of Photofest, Inc.

Peter Criss

audio tracks 70

Here are some sixteenth-note feels with a quarter-note ride pattern:

audio tracks 71

Dave Grohl powered Nirvana's "Smells Like Teen Spirit" with a quarter-note ride on partially open hi-hat cymbals and a sixteenth-note groove between the snare and bass.

Smells Like Teen Sprit

Words and Music by
Kurt Cobain, Krist Novoselic and Dave Grohl

Using a quarter-note ride with eighth-note or sixteenth-note feels can help one "loosen up" the snare and bass drum groove on songs where you want a more relaxed feel. The quarter-note ride will keep the time consistent, but in between the quarter notes, you can play some subdivisions a little more "laid back" or "on top" to give your groove more personality and prevent every note from sounding metronomic.

EIGHTH-NOTE RIDE

An eighth-note ride is probably the most-used ride pattern in rock. Here are just a few of the possibilities:

audio tracks 72

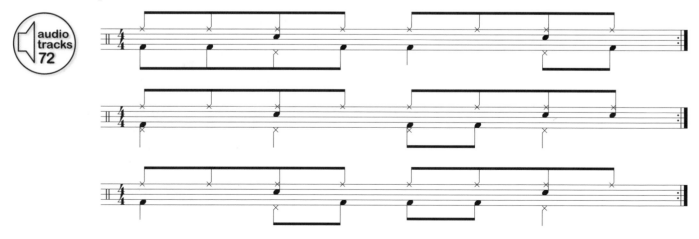

Play all of the previous patterns riding on the closed hi-hat instead of the ride cymbal, omitting the hi-hat pedal part. Then try playing all of the previous patterns with a quarter-note ride.

Stewart Copeland used this eighth-note groove in the pre-chorus of "Message in a Bottle" by The Police.

Message in a Bottle

Music and Lyrics by
Sting

Kenny Aronoff used this two-bar variation of a classic early rock beat on the bridge section of John Cougar Mellencamp's "Hurts So Good."

Hurts So Good

Words and Music by
John Mellencamp and George Green

Here's a basic eighth-note feel that has been used on many songs. Steven Adler used it on "Sweet Child o' Mine" by Guns N' Roses.

Sweet Child O' Mine

Words and Music by W. Axl Rose, Slash,
Izzy Stradlin', Duff McKagan and Steven Adler

Here's a popular two-measure pattern, as used by Al Jackson on the Booker T. & the MG's song "Back Home":

Back Home

By Steve Cropper, Donald Dunn,
Al Jackson, Jr. and Booker T. Jones

Alex Van Halen used this eighth-note groove for Van Halen's "Jump."

Jump

Words and Music by David Lee Roth, Edward Van Halen,
Alex Van Halen and Michael Anthony

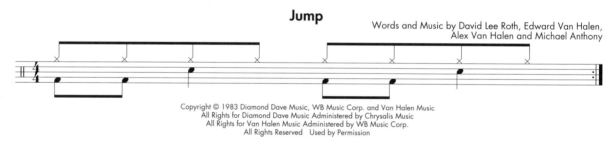

Charlie Watts of the Rolling Stones is famous for leaving out the hi-hat notes on beats 2 and 4 when playing an eighth-note ride. Not only does it help him get his right hand out of the way when slamming left-hand backbeats on the snare, it also opens up the feel a little bit so that the snare backbeats can be a little bit laid back. Here's how he used it on the Stones song "Shattered."

Shattered

Words and Music by
Mick Jagger and Keith Richards

Such drummers as Steve Jordan, Levon Helm, and Jim Keltner have also used Watts's approach, and here's how Kenny Aronoff used it on John Cougar Mellencamp's "Authority Song":

Authority Song

Words and Music by
John Mellencamp

Def Leppard drummer Rick Allen, who lost his left arm in a tragic automobile accident, used the Watts approach so he could play hi-hat and snare drum with the same hand. He added a couple of sixteenths on the bass drum to his basic pattern for "Pour Some Sugar on Me."

Pour Some Sugar on Me

Words and Music by Joe Elliott, Phil Collen, Richard Savage,
Richard Allen, Steve Clark and Robert Lange

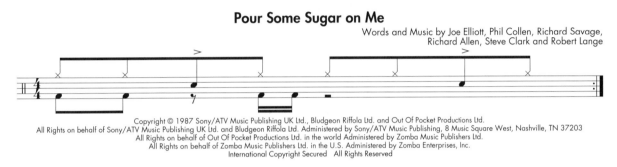

On the Train song "She's on Fire," drummer Scott Underwood created a very open sounding sixteenth-note feel by mixing just a few sixteenths with his eighth-note ride pattern. (Note, the first measure of this two-bar phrase has been used in a *lot* of songs!)

She's on Fire

Words and Music by Pat Monahan, Jimmy Stafford,
Rob Hotchkiss, Charlie Colin and Scott Underwood

On Heart's "Barracuda" drummer Michael Derosier set up a fairly busy sixteenth-note feel between the bass and snare within the framework of an eighth-note ride.

Barracuda

Words and Music by Nancy Wilson, Ann Wilson,
Michael Derosier and Roger Fisher

SIXTEENTH-NOTE RIDE

Sixteenth-note ride patterns are generally used on songs with slower overall tempos; all of those sixteenths help fill out the sound. You can use a sixteenth-note ride pattern on faster songs as well by playing it on a closed hi-hat and alternating the hands, coming off the hi-hat for the snare drum notes (as shown in Chapter 7).

Here are some basic sixteenth-note ride patterns:

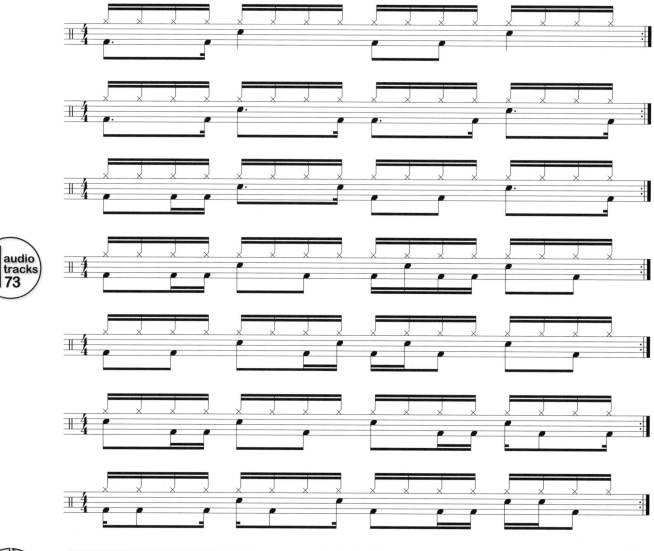

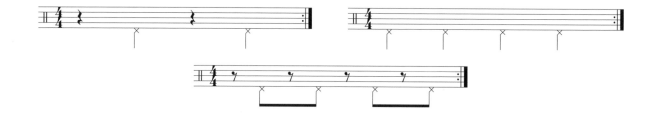

On the previous patterns, substitute ride cymbal for hi-hat and play the following patterns with the hi-hat pedal. To get more of a "rock ballad" sound, play the snare drum notes with a cross-stick technique.

On the Steve Miller Band's song "Swingtown," Gary Mallaber used this alternating sixteenth variation.

Swingtown

Chad Smith of the Red Hot Chili Peppers used an alternating sixteenth-note ride between hi-hat and snare drum on "The Zephyr Song" from the album *By the Way*.

The Zephyr Song

Smith used this variation of a sixteenth-note ride for the Red Hot Chili Peppers' song "Minor Thing."

Minor Thing

CHAPTER 20
PROGRESSIVE ROCK

What's Ahead:
- Well-known drummers
- Progressive rock-styled drum beats

In the late 1960s, a number of bands began playing a style of music that became known as "progressive" rock. This style is aimed more at listeners than dancers, so progressive rock drummers are usually less concerned with slamming backbeats and more interested in coming up with creative, technically challenging drum parts.

There is sometimes a fine line separating progressive rock from fusion, except that fusion, being more associated with jazz, often features a lot more improvisation and is typically instrumental. Progressive rock usually features lyrics, and is often associated with classical music, with more emphasis on composition.

WELL-KNOWN DRUMMERS

Drummers who set the standard for progressive rock performance included Robert Wyatt with Soft Machine; Jon Hiseman with Colosseum; Phil Collins with Genesis; Clive Bunker and Barriemore Barlow with Jethro Tull; Bill Bruford with Yes, King Crimson, and UK; Carl Palmer of ELP (Emerson, Lake & Palmer) and Asia; Phil Ehart of Kansas; Rod Morgenstein with the Dixie Dregs; Neil Peart of Rush; Danny Carey with Tool; and Mike Portnoy of Dream Theater.

PROGRESSIVE ROCK-STYLED DRUM BEATS

Drum parts for progressive rock songs tend to be very integrated with the song itself, meaning that instead of laying down a repetitive pattern for the whole song, or different sections of the song, the drum part will often work very closely with the melody in terms of accenting certain parts of the beat that correspond to the melodic or lyrical structure. So while there will be an overall groove or feel, every measure might be a little different.

As mentioned earlier, progressive rock songs are not aimed at dancers, and thus the song-writers are free to use a variety of time signatures—sometimes changing time signatures from measure to measure within the same song.

Because progressive rock drum parts are tailored to specific songs, it is difficult to come up with generic "prog rock" beats. But here are some patterns based on the work of several progressive rock drummers that will give you an idea of the possibilities.

On the intro to the Foo Fighters' song "Times Like These," Taylor Hawkins delivers a powerful 7/4 groove with a fill at the end.

Times Like These

Words and Music by
Foo Fighters

Here are a couple of measures from "Silent Talking" by Yes, in which Bill Bruford plays a groove in 9/4:

Silent Talking

Words and Music by Jonathan Elias, Jon Anderson,
Steve Howe, Rick Wakeman, and Bill Bruford

This groove can also be thought of as a measure of 4/4, then a measure of 5/4, instead of one long measure of 9/4.

In the Kansas tune "Song for America," drummer Phil Ehart created an interesting linear groove.

Song for America

Words and Music by
Kerry Livgren

In the tune "Watcher of the Skies," (from the Genesis album *Foxtrot*), drummer Phil Collins creates a dynamic groove in 6/4. It starts out by fading in, utilizing mostly the hi-hat. Eventually, the snare and bass drum are added to form the beat shown below. This beat is also played with the ride cymbal instead of the hi-hat.

Watcher of the Skies

Words and Music by Tony Banks, Phil Collins,
Peter Gabriel, Steve Hackett and Mike Rutherford

For the UK song "In the Dead of Night," Bill Bruford created a 7/4 groove that was played very much in the jazz-fusion style in which he maintained a consistent feel without playing a repetitive pattern. Here is an eight-measure sample:

In the Dead of Night

Words and Music by
Eddie Jobson and John Wetton

On the King Crimson track "Frame by Frame," Bruford kept a 7/8 groove on a small auxiliary tom and the snare drum, but underneath, the hi-hat maintained a quarter-note pulse by playing on beats 1, 3, 5, and 7 of the first measure and beats 2, 4, and 6 of the second, in a two-bar pattern.

Photo by Ian Dickson/Redferns Music Picture Library

Bill Bruford

Frame by Frame

Words and Music by William Scott Bruford, Robert Fripp, Tony Levin, and Adrian Belew

CHAPTER 21
FUNK

> **What's Ahead:**
> * Delayed backbeats
> * Sixteenth-note grooves
> * Linear beats

During the 1950s and early '60s, long before anyone was playing what became known as jazz-rock fusion, some jazz musicians began experimenting with a type of syncopated jazz that drew very heavily from blues, and that also had a little bit of rock influence in terms of its rhythmic feel and emphasis on backbeats. This music was often labeled "boogaloo" jazz, and is considered by many to be one of the roots of funk.

Funk also grew out of the "soul" music that became popular in the 1960s with such artists as Aretha Franklin, Booker T. & the MG's, Ray Charles, Wilson Pickett, and, most notably, James Brown. Funk became a major musical force in the 1970s through artists such as the Meters; Chic; Earth, Wind & Fire; Parliament/Funkadelic; Tower of Power; and Sly & the Family Stone; among others. And many "mainstream" artists included funk influences in their music.

DELAYED BACKBEATS

The early funk was fairly simple, characterized by syncopation. Often, one of the backbeats would be delayed to give a "kick" to the beat.

Opening the hi-hat on offbeats also helped create a syncopated feel.

Notice that there is no "plus" sign on the hi-hat note following the open hi-hat note. In most modern drumset notation, it is assumed that, if there is no "circle" above the note, the hi-hat should be closed.

On the two-bar pattern used in James Brown's 1967 hit "Cold Sweat, Pt. 1," drummer Clyde Stubblefield called attention to the "ands" of beats 1 and 3 with an open hi-hat, delayed the backbeat in the first measure to the "and" of four, and left out the bass drum on the first beat of the second measure.

Photo by Robin Little/Redferns Music Picture Library
Clyde Stubblefield

Cold Sweat, Pt. 1

Words and Music by
James Brown and Alfred James Ellis

SIXTEENTH-NOTE GROOVES

As funk developed in the 1970s and '80s, drummers started getting "busier," with almost constant sixteenth notes going between the bass drum and snare drum.

To get a more open sound, drummers sometimes put the sixteenths on the hi-hat. Often, they would play the sixteenths "hand to hand," coming off the hi-hat for snare drum hits.

Many funk drummers got away from playing straight quarters, eighths, or sixteenths on the hi-hat. Here is the pattern David Garibaldi used on the Tower of Power song "Soul Vaccination." Note the "independent" quality between the snare/bass pattern and the hi-hat rhythm.

Soul Vaccination

Words and Music by
Stephen Kupka and Emilio Castillo

LINEAR BEATS

Some funk uses what is known as a *linear* approach. Instead of having separate "parts," such as a continuous ride pattern that is played over a snare drum/bass drum groove (with possibly a constant hi-hat pulse going on underneath all that), you will generally only play one part of the drumkit at a time, using the different drumset voices to create a groove the same way a pianist would combine individual notes on the keyboard to create a melody. This enables you to play fairly "busy" patterns but still have an "open" sound.

With linear funk patterns, the hi-hat or cymbal generally does not play a steady quarter-note or eighth-note ride. Instead, you might get hi-hat only on the offbeats, as in the following two patterns.

In the previous examples, try substituting the bell of the ride cymbal for the hi-hat, and keep a quarter-note pulse with the hi-hat pedal.

You can also "double up" the offbeat like this:

Rick Marotta used that approach on Steely Dan's "Peg," often opening the hi-hat slightly on the second sixteenth note.

Peg

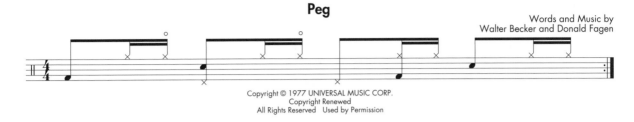

Here are some other linear funk patterns in which the different parts of the drumkit combine to create a groove:

During much of the Living Colour track "Funny Vibe," drummer Will Calhoun played a groove that was mostly linear, with just a few bass/hi-hat combinations. Here's a sample measure:

Funny Vibe

A lot of funk is played with a triplet or shuffle feel, which evolved into the basic hip-hop feel. Here's the funk/hip-hop feel that Jabo Starks played on "Soul Power" by James Brown:

Soul Power

Far-Out Stuff

CHAPTER 22
SPECIAL EFFECT CYMBALS AND DRUMS

> **What's Ahead:**
> - Special effect cymbals
> - Additional drums
> - Electronic pads
> - Additional percussion

In addition to the standard cymbals and drums found on most drumsets, some players like to use "special effect" instruments to add color or alternate sounds to specific tunes. Since these tend to be used only occasionally, they can be mounted a little farther away, but you still need to position them in such a way that reaching for them won't mess up your timing.

SPECIAL EFFECT CYMBALS

Splash

A splash cymbal is a very small crash cymbal. They generally come in 6, 8, 10, and 12 inch sizes. A splash cymbal doesn't have much volume, but it can be quite effective for quick, bright accents.

China

China cymbals (also called Chinese cymbals) are based on the cymbal design used in China, as opposed to the Turkish design that most cymbals are based on. Instead of a rounded bell, the bells on China cymbals are more square-shaped. China cymbals are also turned up at the edges.

The most popular China cymbals are 18 or 20 inches in diameter, but you can also find 16 and 22 inch Chinas. China cymbals generally have a lot of dark overtones, which many drummers describe as "trashy" sounding. (But to people who love that sound, "trashy" is a compliment!)

Smaller Chinas are often used as crash cymbals, while larger ones tend to be used as rides. In either case, many drummers mount them upside-down so that the turned-up edge won't cut into drumsticks.

Sizzle

A sizzle cymbal has several rivets, which add some shimmer to the cymbal sound, and also increase the sustain. Most often, drummers use rivets in ride cymbals rather than in crash cymbals.

Most sizzle cymbals have either six or eight rivets spread out around the circumference of the cymbal. Using too many rivets can muffle the sound of the cymbal, and having too many holes in a cymbal can seriously weaken it.

Some jazz drummers, such as Louie Bellson and Peter Erskine, like to have just three rivets mounted in a cymbal, and they put them rather close together in a triangular pattern. It produces a gentle sizzle sound that is especially nice when you are playing with brushes and want a delicate crash sound.

Be very careful about drilling holes in your cymbal for mounting rivets. If the drill bit gets too hot, it can damage the tempering of the cymbal metal and ruin its sound. Drilling holes incorrectly can also cause a cymbal to crack. Either take the cymbal to someone at a music store or drum shop who has experience drilling holes in cymbals, or at the very least get advice from someone who has done it.

You can buy a device called a "sizzler" that can be mounted above the bell of a cymbal. It has two "arms" with rivets on the ends, and the arms can be quickly lowered so that the rivets bounce against the cymbal when it is played, or raised so the rivets do not contact the cymbal. Many drummers prefer using this rather than drilling holes in their cymbal. It also gives you the option of having a sizzle cymbal for certain songs and a regular cymbal for other songs, without having to have two different cymbals in your setup.

Another way to get a sizzle effect is to get a length of beaded chain (like they often use on a sink-drain stopper), loop it around the wing nut on your cymbal stand, and let the chain lay across the cymbal. That will produce a very similar sound to rivets and, again, you don't have to drill any holes in your cymbal.

Cymbal companies got the idea for putting rivets into cymbals from jazz drummers such as Art Blakey, who used to hang a key ring over the wing nut of his ride cymbal so that the metal keys would vibrate against the cymbal when he played.

Swish

A swish cymbal is simply a China cymbal with rivets. As with sizzle cymbals, six or eight rivets is usually enough. If you have more, the cymbal's natural sound will be muffled, and too many holes in a cymbal will weaken it.

Flatride

A flatride is a ride cymbal that does not have a bell. They are generally used by jazz drummers to provide a delicate ride sound that has good definition, but flatrides turn up in other settings as well; for example, Charlie Watts of the Rolling Stones often has a flatride in his setup.

Stacked Cymbals: Mounting Two Cymbals Together

Some drummers (notably Terry Bozzio) will sometimes mount two cymbals together, one on top of the other, which produces a very dry, "white noise" effect. Often, a larger cymbal is mounted on top of a slightly smaller one so that the smaller cymbal fits inside the bell of the larger one (pictured left, below). Other times, drummers will mount a regular splash inside a China splash (pictured right). It's just one of those things you have to experiment with based on the cymbals you have available.

CD Track 87 contains audio examples of the following cymbals, in this order: splash, China, sizzle, flatride, and two cymbals mounted togehter (stacked cymbals).

ADDITIONAL DRUMS

Auxiliary Snare Drums

If you don't want the same snare drum sound on every song, you can add an auxiliary snare drum. Most drummers mount them to the left of their main snare drum. Some drummers put them behind the hi-hat so that they have to twist a bit to the left to hit it; other drummers put the auxiliary snare drum in front of the hi-hat, to the left of the small tom. But you can put it wherever you want, based on the size of your set and how much you plan to use it.

There can also be a very practical reason for having an auxiliary snare drum. If you tend to break a lot of snare drum heads, it can be handy to have another drum already sitting there that you can switch to until the end of the set, when you can change the head on your main drum.

The most popular auxiliary snare drums are *piccolo snares*. They come in a variety of sizes, with 3 x 13 and 3 x 14 being the most popular. Piccolo snare drums are generally tuned to produce a very high-pitched "crack." With their shallow shells, they don't have a full-bodied sound, but the high pitch helps them cut through a band's volume.

Different manufacturers make various snare drums with a variety of names. Some are called soprano drums, and usually have 10 or 12 inch heads. To make up for the small head sizes, such drums often have deeper shells than piccolo drums, but as the head size gets smaller, you need to be careful about too much depth or the drum will have a "hollow" sound (sometimes called the "coffee-can effect"). If the snares are too far away from the top head you will not get fast snare response, and the drum will sound more like a tom-tom with snares than an actual snare drum.

What you use for an auxiliary snare drum depends a lot on what you use for your main snare drum. Drummers who use standard 5 x 14 or 6 1/2 x 14 snare drums usually go for smaller auxiliary snare drums, but some drummers do just the opposite and use a thin, high-pitched snare (a piccolo, a 4 x 14, or even a 5 x 14 tuned high) as their main drum, and then go for a much deeper drum on the side.

There are no rules here. Decide what sounds your music requires, and what sounds you like to play, and then choose whatever drums suit your needs. But if you are going to use an extra snare drum, make sure it is different enough in sound to make a real difference.

Toms

It can be difficult to say where "regular" toms leave off and "auxiliary" toms begin, but generally speaking, extremely large or extremely small toms would be considered "extras" by most drummers, as you would tend to use them less often. The most useful auxiliary toms are small ones, with 6 and 8 inch head sizes. They can add a lot of color to certain songs, and because they are so small, they can more easily be incorporated into a setup. Extra large toms, by contrast, take up a lot of room, and because their pitch is so low, they don't cut through very well and start getting into the bass drum's tonal range. So if you want some extra toms for effects or for melodic patterns, small drums with higher pitches will usually do you more good.

Timbales

Timbales are Afro-Cuban instruments that resemble one-headed toms and generally feature metal shells. They produce a brighter sound than standard toms. They generally come in pairs and are mounted on a floor stand. If you do a lot of Latin or reggae tunes, a timbale or two can provide a more "authentic" sound to your fills.

ELECTRONIC PADS

Different types of electronic pads are available that can each get a variety of sounds, from different drum and percussion colors to a variety of sound effects. Some drummers use a single electronic pad for sounds that they only need occasionally. For example, for one song, the pad can be programmed for a piccolo snare drum sound; on another song, it can be set to sound like a woodblock; for yet a different song, it can sound like a gong; and for a special effect on a different tune, it can sound like glass breaking.

There are also pad sets that contain several playing surfaces all mounted in a single unit, which allows you to have several different sounds available at the same time. You can also set each pad to the same type of sound but give each one a different pitch so that you can play melodic patterns.

Pad sets such as the Roland SPD20 offer multiple playing surfaces and hundreds of sounds and effects.

See Chapter 28, Electronic Kits, for more on electronics that can be incorporated into a drumset.

ADDITIONAL PERCUSSION

Even before world music became influential, many drummers included small percussion instruments in their setups.

Cowbells are probably the single most popular percussion add-on, and they've been popular with drumset players for many years. They don't take up much room and can be a nice alternative to a ride cymbal or hi-hat for heavy rock or Latin tunes.

See Chapter 14, Latin and World Percussion, for more on percussion instruments that can be incorporated into a drumset.

CHAPTER 23

EXTENDED TECHNIQUES AND SPECIAL EFFECTS

What's ahead:
- Rimshot variations
- Drum rolls
- Ghost notes
- Hi-hat splash
- Playing with the hands
- Bowing cymbals
- Changing drum pitches
- Junk
- Playing outside the time

RIMSHOT VARIATIONS

A rimshot involves striking the rim of the drum and the drumhead simultaneously with the same stick. The resulting sound is generally sharper, brighter, and more cutting than that made when simply striking the drumhead. The technique is most often used on the snare drum, and is frequently employed by rock, pop, and blues drummers when playing the loud backbeats that characterize that music. Rimshots are also employed on tom-toms (or timbales) in Afro-Cuban and reggae music, giving a bright, metallic quality to the notes. The standard rimshot is played by bringing the stick down so that the shoulder, or shaft, of the stick strikes the rim at the same time the tip, or bead, of the stick strikes the drumhead.

Cross-stick

A popular variation of the rimshot is the cross-stick, in which the tip of the stick rests on the drumhead and the stick is pivoted so that its shoulder strikes the rim, producing a bright "pop" sound. The cross-stick technique is frequently used to simulate the sound of claves in styles such as the Brazilian bossa nova, and it is also popular among rock, pop, and country drummers for ballads.

Stick-shot

Another rimshot variation is the stick-shot, in which the tip of one stick rests on the head with its shoulder resting on the rim, and is struck by the other stick.

Rim Click

A rim click involves simply striking the rim of the drum. Some refer to this as a rimshot, but a true rimshot involves striking both the rim and the head at the same time.

DRUM ROLLS

A drum roll consists of a series of strokes played so close together as to simulate a single long tone. Rolls can be "closed," meaning that the strokes are extremely close together, or "open," meaning that the individual strokes are more apparent.

Double-stroke rolls are associated with the rudimental tradition and are performed by playing two strokes (i.e., a double stroke) with each hand in quick succession, ending the roll with a single tap. Short rolls are often designated by the number of strokes—5-stroke roll, 7-stroke roll, 9-

stroke roll, and so on. Double-stroke rolls are especially appropriate for deep field drums that require a more powerful stroke. In rudimental settings, double-stroke rolls are generally played as thirty-second notes. But drumset players sometimes use double-stroke rolls on tom-toms because toms tend to have looser batter heads that do not respond as well to multiple-bounce rolls. (See Chapter 24, Drum Rudiments, for more on double-stroke rolls.)

Multiple-bounce rolls (also called *buzz rolls*) are played by pressing the drumsticks into the drumhead in quick succession so that each stroke produces a smooth series of bounces. Bounce rolls are most typically used by orchestral percussionists and jazz drummers, as well as by Scottish pipe-band drummers performing on modern, high-tension side drums. Although bounce rolls can be played on any drum, they are most often used on the snare drum, where the vibration of the snares helps sustain the sound. A popular guideline among drummers is to make a multiple-bounce roll sound like the tearing of sandpaper. Before the advent of ride cymbals, early jazz drummers such as Baby Dodds kept time on a snare drum with short "press" rolls, which were played as tight multiple-bounce rolls.

Rolls are indicated by slashes through the stem of a note. In the following example, the first roll begins on beat 2 and ends on beat 3; the second roll begins on beat 4 and ends on beat 1 of the second measure; the next roll starts on beat 3 and ends on beat 4; and the final roll (the half-note roll) begins on beat 3 of measure three and ends on beat 1 of the last measure.

At a medium tempo, you would play those rolls by playing sixteenth notes as multiple-bounce strokes. The following example shows how the previous example would be played. A "Z" through a stem indicates a multiple-bounce stroke.

At a slightly faster tempo, you might play triplets instead of sixteenth notes.

At an even faster tempo, you would play the rolls as eighth-note multiple-bounce strokes.

Single-stroke rolls consist of rapidly alternating individual strokes and are best suited to drums that produce sustained tones, such as tom-toms. Rock and pop music drumset players typically use single-stroke rolls to go "around the kit" in fills and solos.

GHOST NOTES

Ghost notes can be played on any drum or cymbal, but are most often played on snare drum or hi-hat. They are played so softly that listeners may not be sure they are even hearing them. They are usually indicated by parentheses.

If listeners can barely hear them, then why play them? One reason that drummers often play them is for the benefit of the feel. Let's say that you are playing a New Orleans-type groove with the following basic rhythm.

There is a lot of space between those notes, which can throw off the timing. Also, just playing those notes doesn't always create a sense of flow. But if you played it by accenting the main notes and playing the notes in-between the accents as ghost notes, as shown below, it will help ensure a steady time flow and give the music more momentum.

Some drummers like to throw in ghost notes when playing shuffle patterns between the snare and hi-hat.

Subtleties such as ghost notes add a lot of character and expression to your music. Even though the notes are very soft, and many listeners might not be consciously aware that you are playing them, they will subconsciously hear them and they will find your playing to be more interesting, even if they don't know why.

HI-HAT SPLASH

This technique emulates the sound of a pair of hand cymbals being crashed together, except where hand-cymbal crashes are usually explosive, a hi-hat splash is a fairly delicate sound.

To achieve this effect, bring the hi-hat cymbals together with the pedal, but instead of holding the pedal down to get the normal "chick" sound, immediately let the pedal back up so that the cymbals can vibrate freely.

A hi-hat splash is generally notated with a small "o" underneath the hi-hat pedal note.

PLAYING WITH THE HANDS

For a change of texture, try putting the sticks aside and playing with your bare hands. Jazz drummer Joe Morello sometimes played solos with his hands when he was with the Dave Brubeck Quartet, and rock drumming icon John Bonham did the same with Led Zeppelin. Some drummers like to play with their hands during Latin-style songs to imitate the sound of congas and bongos. Be careful, however! Keep your hands on the drumheads; do not collide with metal rims or cymbals because you can injure yourself.

But I don't mean to scare you away from trying some bare-handed playing. Getting that stick out from between you and the drum can make you feel more connected with your instrument (which is why many drummers are drawn to hand drums such as djembes and congas). By using different parts of your hands (fingertips, palms, various combinations of fingers), you can get a wide variety of sounds from a single drum.

Unless you are in a small room with good acoustics or you are miked very well, many of the nuances you can achieve with your hands will be lost. But in the right situation, playing with the hands can add a great deal of expression to your playing.

BOWING CYMBALS

You can get a really eerie sound by drawing a violin (or viola, cello, bass, etc.) bow across the edge of a cymbal. Obviously, this fits into the category of "extreme" special effects, as you can't very well incorporate such a technique into the typical groove—but for a certain type of song, it might be the perfect effect.

Getting the right touch and pressure can take some experimenting, so be patient. (You might want to seek advice from a string player.) And scraping a bow across a cymbal can be pretty hard on the bowhair, so don't borrow someone's good bow for your experiments. Check with a music store that deals in string instruments to see if they have an old bow they will let you have cheap. And don't forget the rosin (you need that to get resistance so the cymbal will vibrate).

CHANGING DRUM PITCHES

You can often get an African talking-drum effect on tom-toms by pressing into the head with one hand as you play it with the other hand. As you press into the head, the pitch goes up, and depending on how your drum is tuned and how flexible your drumhead is, you might be able to get a fairly decent range of pitches. (If the head is tuned too tight, you won't have much range. So if this is something you plan to do a lot, tune your heads on the loose side.)

Instead of pressing with the fingers, some drummers press a drumstick into the head, but if you do that, be sure to use the blunt butt end of the stick rather than the pointed playing end, so you don't poke a hole in your drumhead. Some drummers like to press down on the head with their elbow, which creates an interesting visual effect.

JUNK

You don't have to restrict yourself to items that are manufactured commercially and marketed as "percussion." Some drummers create their own special effect with common household items. I've seen metal garbage can lids mounted like cymbals, hubcaps suspended like gongs, plastic pails used as drums, and soft-drink cans filled with dried beans used as shakers. Steve Gadd once played brushes on a cardboard box and slapped his thighs on a Rickie Lee Jones record called "Woody and Dutch," and Hal Blaine used a plastic water jug to get a unique sound on the Beach Boys' song "Caroline No."

So, the next time you want a unique sound, don't run to the music store to buy something a lot of other people have, and don't fiddle with the sounds on a synthesizer. Go out to the garage (or to a junkyard) and start hitting things. You may be amazed at the sounds you discover.

PLAYING OUTSIDE THE TIME

Although a drummer's primary job is usually defined as "keeping time," drummers do not, in fact, always have to do that. In some cases, the drummer's task is to "color" the music rather than keep the beat. Often this is done in slow, lyrical ballads in which the other musicians are creating a very "flowing" feel. Sharp, staccato drum hits don't work very well in that type of situation, so drummers tend to look for ways to play longer notes and delicate colors that will better complement what the other musicians are doing.

But playing "outside" the time doesn't just happen in ballads. Jazz musicians sometimes play "free," which generally means that the drummer is not expected to maintain a time feel. Free playing is very "impressionistic," being more about creating a mood than about making people dance. (I'm reminded of hearing someone approach a jazz musician between sets at a club one night and asking, "Are you guys playing free jazz?" The musician responded, "No, we're getting paid.")

Rolls are a wonderful way to color a song. You can certainly play rolls with drumsticks, especially on the snare drum, but you might want to check out some alternative mallets as well. For example, by using timpani mallets on tom-toms, you can sound almost like a timpanist and give the music a lot of drama. Timpani mallets can also be used on cymbals for rolls and special effects.

But if you are going to be playing exclusively on the cymbals, you should invest in a pair of yarn mallets like the ones marimba players use. They come in different hardnesses, so for cymbal playing, go for soft or medium-soft. Brushes are also very effective on cymbals when playing freely. You can play single-stroke rolls on different cymbals to create delicate colors, and drummers will sometimes flip their brushes around and gently scrape the metal handle across a cymbal for a shimmering texture.

When freely coloring the music, the drummer does not have to maintain a pulse or time feel. Notes are often played at random, serving as gentle musical punctuation. Quick flurries of notes can also be effective. There are no particular rules here, except the rule that applies whenever you are playing with others: listen to the music and play something that fits.

Playing outside of the time calls on every bit of your musicianship. You can't get away with just being a human metronome and pounding out a beat. You really have to listen so that your playing enhances the music. For starters, don't overdo it. Think of your drum and percussion colors as spices, remembering that a little bit of spice enhances the flavor but too much spice ruins it.

You don't always have to hold back, though. One of the most important musical principles is *tension and release*, which involves contrasts. At times, you may want play to frantic, busy, and possibly loud rolls and flurries of notes. But you probably won't want to do that through the entire tune. Build up to one or more climaxes, and then release them. Listeners will appreciate the loud, busy playing more if it is contrasted with delicate, spacious playing.

When playing "free," by all means follow the other musicians—but take your turns leading, too. If the music is starting to sound boring, add some fireworks. In most cases, you will want to build the intensity gradually, but sometimes a sudden explosion can be just the thing to kick a tune up to the next level. Just be sure that your percussive outbursts are serving the music, not just calling attention to you.

Even when playing free, it's good to restrict yourself to certain sounds and effects for specific tunes. If the idea is to create a mood, then choose sounds and rhythmic phrases that reinforce that mood. For example, for a dramatic mood you might emphasize low, dark, drum sounds. For a delicate mood you might focus on soft cymbal colors. Don't just go wild and throw in everything you can think of. Give each piece its own personality.

CHAPTER 24
DRUM RUDIMENTS

What's Ahead:
- Roll Rudiments
- Diddle Rudiments
- Flam Rudiments
- Drag Rudiments

Often called the "building blocks of drumming" and equated with the scales played on melodic instruments, drum rudiments consist of short rhythmic phrases with specific stickings. Rudiments first developed in the military bands of the 1800s, in which instruction was by rote, and as a result, many rudiments were given names that reflected the way they were played and the sound they made. For example, the long roll was called the "daddy mammy" to reflect its right-right left-left sticking, and the name "flam" imitated the combined sound of a grace note and a primary note. Popular rudiments include the paradiddle, flam accent, ratamacue, and various numbered rolls (i.e., 5-stroke roll, 9-stroke roll, and so on).

The first set of standardized drum rudiments was created by the National Association of Rudimental Drummers (NARD) in 1933, and consisted of 26 rudiments that were considered essential by its members. The Percussive Arts Society (PAS) expanded this set in 1984 by compiling a list of 40 International Drum Rudiments, which included the original 26 NARD rudiments, along with drum corps, European, orchestral, and contemporary snare drum rudiments that had become popular, such as Swiss Army Triplets and the Pataflafla.

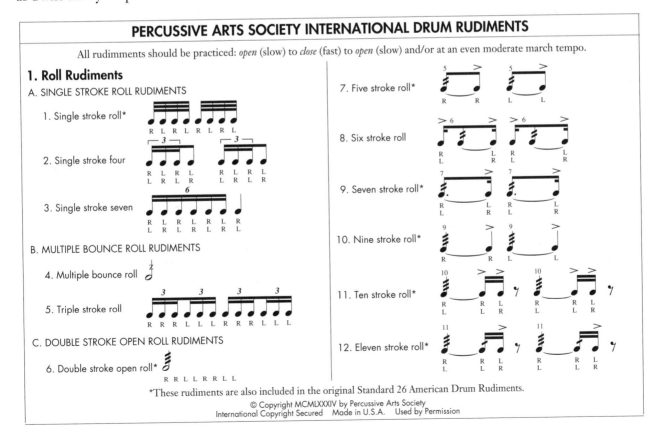

PERCUSSIVE ARTS SOCIETY INTERNATIONAL DRUM RUDIMENTS

All rudiments should be practiced: *open* (slow) to *close* (fast) to *open* (slow) and/or at an even moderate march tempo.

1. Roll Rudiments

A. SINGLE STROKE ROLL RUDIMENTS

1. Single stroke roll*
2. Single stroke four
3. Single stroke seven

B. MULTIPLE BOUNCE ROLL RUDIMENTS

4. Multiple bounce roll
5. Triple stroke roll

C. DOUBLE STROKE OPEN ROLL RUDIMENTS

6. Double stroke open roll*

7. Five stroke roll*
8. Six stroke roll
9. Seven stroke roll*
10. Nine stroke roll*
11. Ten stroke roll*
12. Eleven stroke roll*

*These rudiments are also included in the original Standard 26 American Drum Rudiments.

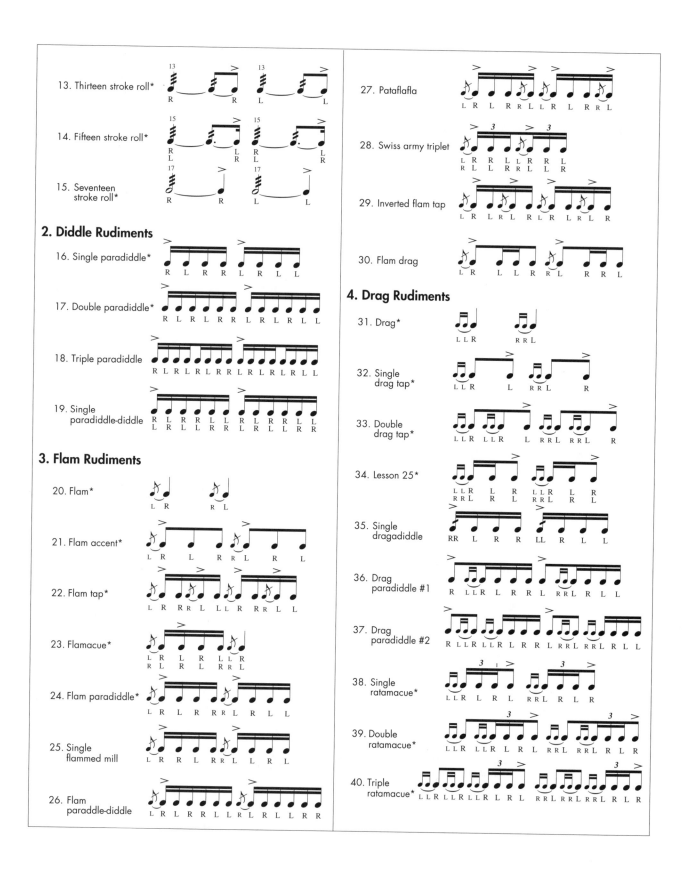

Rudiments are primarily used in military, marching, and drum corps settings, and popular snare drum solos have been written entirely based on rudiments (for example, "The Downfall of Paris" and "The Three Camps"). Although rudiments are considered foundational for various kinds of percussion study, they are sometimes thought to be inessential by drumset players (hence their inclusion in the "Far-out" section of this book). Still, many drumset players use rudiments for technique development, and adapt rudiments to other styles of music. Jazz drummers such as Buddy Rich and Joe Morello often displayed a rudimental influence, while rock drummer Spencer Dryden played a rudimental-style snare drum introduction on Jefferson Airplane's 1960s hit "White Rabbit." Here is Steve Gadd's drum groove from Paul Simon's 1970s hit "50 Ways to Leave Your Lover," which is rudiment-based:

Fifty Ways to Leave Your Lover

Words and Music by
Paul Simon

Copyright © 1975 (Renewed) Paul Simon (BMI)
International Copyright Secured   All Rights Reserved
Used by Permission

Here's how drummer Frank Beard used drag rudiments on the ZZ Top song "Lowdown in the Street":

Lowdown in the Street

Words and Music by
Billy F Gibbons, Dusty Hill and Frank Beard

Copyright © 1982 Stage Three Songs
All Rights Controlled and Administered by Stage Three Music (U.S.) Inc.
All Rights Reserved   Used by Permission

Paradiddles have a lot of drumset applications. Some drummers like to use them for fill and solo patterns to avoid awkward stickings. Here are some basic exercises to get you started.

You can also use paradiddles to create a Latin-sounding groove. Use the bell of the ride cymbal for a more Latin-like sound, or substitute a cowbell. You can also use a cross-stick stroke for the snare drum notes. If you do that, you can play the tom notes with the butt end of the stick so you don't have to flip it over.

There are many other ways to incorporate rudiments into drumset playing. In fact, Peter Magadini wrote an entire book devoted to that topic, called *The Complete Drumset Rudiments*, published by Hal Leonard Corporation.

Song Transcriptions

WALK THIS WAY

Essentially, this is simple classic rock. But the little variations that Aerosmith drummer Joey Kramer added to the fundamental groove gave the song a funky feel, and the sixteenth-note offbeats on the bass drum perfectly complemented the syncopated rhythmic feel of the lyrics. Note how the drum part has a slightly different feel under the guitar solos, with less syncopation, providing solid support.

Walk This Way

Words and Music by
Steven Tyler and Joe Perry

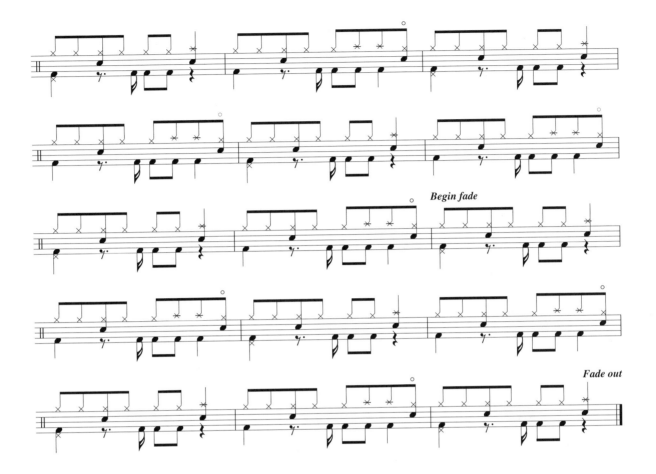

Begin fade

Fade out

NO REPLY AT ALL

This classic song by Genesis has a light, pop-rock sound, but drummer Phil Collins keeps the drum part interesting with a mostly linear approach to the groove, maintaining an eighth-note feel without keeping straight eighths on any single part of the kit. In the verses, he achieves a very open sound by playing a minimum of bass drum notes and by dropping out the hi-hat at the beginning of each measure. Although the part is fairly busy, it never sounds cluttered. At the beginning of the breakdown, he keeps a gentle backbeat on hi-hat before kicking up the intensity with hi-hat sixteenths, but keeps the sound light and flowing by incorporating just a few well-chosen drum hits.

No Reply at All

Words and Music by
Tony Banks, Phil Collins, and Mike Rutherford

SMOKE ON THE WATER

Rock drumming doesn't get much heavier than Ian Paice's performance on this classic by Deep Purple. But Paice also proved that heavy rock drumming could be lifted above the Neanderthal bashing that many people associate with the style through his use of sixteenth, eighth, and quarter note feels to drive different sections of the tune, as well as by his subtle use of open hi-hat colors and snare drum ghost notes. And check out the drums-only backing of the guitar solo.

Smoke on the Water

Words and Music by Ritchie Blackmore, Ian Gillan, Roger Glover, Jon Lord, and Ian Paice

Play 6 times

Verse

3. We end-ed up at the Grand Ho-tel,_____

it was emp - ty, cold and bare. But with the Roll-ing truck Stones thing

CISSY STRUT

This is one of the all-time funk classics, originally recorded by the Meters featuring drummer Joseph "Zigaboo" Modeliste. The linear groove requires a lot of precision, but it can't be metronomic. Modeliste gave it a loose feel that created an incredible groove. This is all about feel!

Cissy Strut

By Arthur Neville, Leo Nocentelli,
George Porter and Joseph Modeliste, Jr.

NICE TO KNOW YOU

On this tune originally recorded by Incubus, drummer Jose Pasillas made use of a variety of sounds and rhythms to enhance the different sections of the tune and to keep the song interesting throughout. This chart has it all, from a delicate cymbal/cross-stick groove at the beginning to straight-out bashing in alternating time signatures. This one will take some work, but it will be worth it!

Nice to Know You

Words and Music by Brandon Boyd, Michael Einziger, Alex Katunich, Jose Pasillas II, and Chris Kilmore

Verse

2nd time, substitute Fill 1

1. Bet - ter than watch - ing the Gel - ler bend -
2. — Deep - er than the deep - est Cou -

ing sil - ver spoons.
steau would ev - er go.

And Bet - ter than wit - ness - ing new - born
high - er than the heights of what

— neb - u - laes in bloom.
we of - ten think we know.

See who sees from 'up high'
Blessed she who clear - ly sees

— smiles and sure - ly sings.
— the wood for the trees.

Fill 1

So could it be

that it has been there all a - long? Yeah.

gradually open

Pre-Chorus

I have-n't felt

the way I feel to - day in so long

it's hard for me to spec - i - fy. I'm be-gin-ning to no -

tice how much this feels like a wak - ing limb.... pins and nee -

Chorus

dles, nice to know you, good - bye!

The Gig

CHAPTER 25
PERFORMANCE ETIQUETTE

What's Ahead:
- What to wear
- What to bring
- Show up on time
- Stay in your place
- Be dependable
- Recommendations

WHAT TO WEAR

Every gig and every type of music has its own set of rules. For some types of gigs, you are expected to wear formal attire. For other gigs, jeans and a T-shirt is considered proper attire.

The important thing is to know what's expected in whatever situation you will be working in. If someone is calling you for a gig and you're not sure what to wear, ask. No one will think less of you for checking on the dress code, but if you show up in the wrong clothes, you will not be regarded as professional.

If you are required to "dress up," make sure that your dress clothes fit in such a way to allow you to play comfortably. You may want a looser fitting suit or tux than normal to accommodate the kinds of "moves" a drummer needs to make. Try playing in your dress attire before you go to the gig, so you don't find out when you're on stage that your clothes are too tight for playing. You'll either play badly, tear your favorite suit, or both!

WHAT TO BRING

The same goes for your equipment. Make sure you have the right drums and cymbals for the job. If you are playing a wedding reception with a standard variety band, don't haul in a double-bass kit with eight power toms and a dozen cymbals. And don't take a four-piece kit with a 20-inch bass drum to a hard rock gig.

If you specialize in one style of music, you can probably use the same drums and cymbals for everything. But if you are looking to work in a variety of situations, you may need some different equipment for different types of gigs.

SHOW UP ON TIME

My favorite quote about being professional came from legendary studio drummer Gary Chester, who said, "If I knew for sure that the world was going to end at 2:00, and I had a session booked for 1:00, *I'd be there!*"

An important part of being professional is showing up on time, and for a drummer that means showing up early enough that you have plenty of time to get all of your equipment inside and set up. If you are playing somewhere you have never played before, show up extra early because you never know what kinds of obstacles you might run into in terms of loading-in your equipment.

Another reason for drummers to arrive early is that we need some space when we are setting up—room to get multiple drums and cymbals out of cases, room to set up stands or rack systems, and room to assemble everything into a nice, compact drumset. If other musicians are already on the stage and there are amplifiers and other pieces of equipment taking up floor space, getting drums set up becomes more difficult. Personally, I like being the first musician there so I have plenty of time and space to set up (and then warm up) before the stage starts getting crowded. It's also a good idea, when possible, to have everything set up before the audience starts coming in. Ideally, they should only see you playing, not constructing your drumset, tuning it, or warming up.

Keep in mind that unforeseen things can delay you, so be sure to allow a little extra travel time. It's much better to arrive too early than to arrive too late. The scariest situation I had was one summer when I was doing a gig on a nightly riverboat cruise. One evening as I was heading for the gig, I heard on the radio that there was a traffic accident on the bridge I usually crossed to get to the boat landing, and the bridge was temporarily closed. So I immediately changed routes and headed for the other bridge that would get me across the river. Of course, a lot of other people also headed for that bridge—which was down to one lane because of construction. Even though traffic was moving, it was moving very slowly. I could see the riverboat from the bridge, and suddenly had the horrible realization that if I didn't get there in time, the gig would take off down the river without me. Fortunately, I made it in time. And, luckily, most of my kit was already set up on the stage; I was only carrying a stick bag and a cymbal bag. But the only reason I made it on time was because I was in the habit of getting to the gig early, so I had some time to work with when I encountered the delay.

STAY IN YOUR PLACE

With certain types of gigs—such as many wedding receptions, dances, and private parties—the musicians are expected to be seen only on stage and nowhere else. You may be required to set up your equipment during the afternoon so that you don't disturb the guests by hauling in your stuff while they are having dinner. Or there might be a certain door you are expected to use that leads directly to the performance area. During breaks, you might be expected to stay in a dressing room. In such situations, you are not one of the "guests," and you will not be treated like "stars of the show." You are part of the "hired help," like the caterer, and you need to behave accordingly. Do not help yourself to food or drink unless invited to do so. And even then, find out where you are allowed to sit and eat. There might be a table set aside for the musicians, but you might be asked to eat backstage or in the kitchen.

BE DEPENDABLE

Once you have accepted a gig, don't back out unless it is an absolute emergency. Don't cancel a gig just because someone called later with another offer that paid a little better. Word gets around, and if you back out of too many gigs, you'll get a reputation as the drummer who is going to "bail."

Granted, sometimes a second offer comes along that you can't refuse. For example, you accept a one-nighter, but then someone else offers you an entire week. If you are trying to make a living playing drums, you might need to cancel the one-nighter for a week's worth of work.

But even then, consider it carefully. Does the person who hired you for the one-night gig give you a lot of regular work? Will the full-week job lead to other work, or are you just filling in for someone in a situation where it's likely you will never be called to play with this band again? Be careful about blowing off someone who hires you frequently. Loyalty means a lot.

By the same token, most musicians have been in similar situations and will be understanding. The more notice you are able to give, the more chance that the person who hired you for the first job will have time to find someone else. You might offer to recommend another drummer if he doesn't know anyone. But don't ever cancel at the last minute and leave a leader without a drummer. You will destroy your own reputation by doing that.

RECOMMENDATIONS

I once heard someone say, "Other drummers don't hire you for gigs; piano players, guitar players, and trumpet players hire you, so those are the people you need to become friends with." Yes, other drummers don't tend to hire you, but they often recommend you, so you do, in fact, need to be friendly with other drummers. These drummers include people who play the same style(s) as you—those who you can feel good about recommending to someone if you are not available, and who might be able to recommend you to someone else.

When making a recommendation, always recommend someone who is at least as good as you and maybe even a little better. Don't recommend an inferior drummer out of fear that if you recommend a good drummer, the contractor will like that drummer so much that you will never get called again. The contractor will appreciate the fact that you gave a good recommendation and be more likely to call you again than if you stuck him with a lousy drummer. Also, the contractor will likely tell the other drummer that he got the recommendation from you, and that other drummer will probably return the favor at some point. Good drummers are going to get more calls than bad drummers, and they will, therefore, be more likely to need to recommend people for the gigs they can't cover. So recommending good drummers pays off in more than one way.

CHAPTER 26
ON THE JOB

What's Ahead:
* Warming up
* Showmanship
* Faking it
* Equipment failures
* Backups
* Preventive maintenance
* Backup essentials

WARMING UP

You don't want to go on stage "cold," without having warmed up your playing muscles. Not only will you feel stiff for the first song or two, but you can actually damage muscles and tendons by over-exerting them without a proper warm-up period. Remember, there is an athletic quality to playing drums, so you want to prepare for a gig the same way that athletes prepare for a game: by warming up.

The best way to warm up your playing muscles is to use them the same way you will be using them when you play. Ideally, you should sit behind your kit and run through some simple beats and fills. But that's not always possible or desirable. Ideally, an audience should not have to listen to band members warm up or tune. That should all be done backstage or in a dressing room. The audience should only hear the music.

Guitar players have no problem having their instrument with them offstage so they can warm up. But you can't drag your drumset into a dressing room and then drag it back to the stage when it's time to play. Therefore, many drummers carry a practice pad with them so they can easily (and quietly) get their hands and arms moving before it's time to play. Some drummers even have entire practice-pad drumkits set up in the dressing room so they can warm up as realistically as possible.

At the very least, carry a small pad with you so you can warm up your hands. Small pads are available that you can strap around your thigh so you can warm up on your leg without hurting yourself. And just tapping your feet on the floor can actually do a pretty good job of getting you ready to play bass drum and hi-hat.

Remember that the purpose of warming up is to get blood flowing into the muscles that you will be using, in order to lubricate them. If you try to play too fast too soon, your muscles will tense up, which will restrict the blood flow. So start out slowly and relaxed. Play some single strokes at a moderate tempo. Gradually speed up, but at the first sign of tension or tightness, back off a little and let your muscles relax.

Doing some simple stretching exercises can also help get your body ready for playing. Don't wear yourself out with your warm-up routine, however; save your energy for the show. (See Chapter 3 for more on warming up.)

SHOWMANSHIP

On some gigs, the band is hired as background music, and so you don't want to do anything that will call attention to you or the band. Just play the music as well as you can and forget any visual elements.

With other gigs, you will be expected to contribute a visual element as well as good playing. For starters, look like you're into it; don't sit there looking bored. Smiling never hurts, but if you're not a natural smiler, look intense or at least interested.

Drummers can't run around a stage the way singers and guitar players can. We're pretty much stuck on our thrones. But our instrument is pretty spread out, and we are in constant motion, especially when we play fills and hit cymbal crashes. So make the most of it. Don't ever make such large movements that they interfere with your timing, but give people something to look at—especially if you are playing in a large room and some of the audience members are pretty far away.

Some drummers like to throw their drumsticks out into the crowd after a show. But people have been injured by flying drumsticks and drummers have been sued. Instead of hurling a stick out into the crowd as far as you can (where someone might not be able to see it coming in the dark), make eye contact with someone close to the stage and toss the stick into his or her hands.

FAKING IT

A lot of things can go wrong during a performance, ranging from someone forgetting what to play to equipment breaking. Hardly a gig goes by that something unforeseen doesn't happen, but professionals know how to cover up a lot of it so that the audience never knows anything happened.

For drummers, the two most common problems involve sticks breaking or flying out of your hands, and drumheads breaking. In either case, don't panic—and don't stop playing! The most important thing for the drummer is to keep the time feel going, but if you suddenly have one less stick or one less drum to work with, you will have to do some fast thinking and adjusting. We will talk about specific situations and how to deal with them below, but the general rule to keep in mind no matter what happens is that you have to prioritize what you are playing, and keep the most important parts going.

For example, let's say a stick breaks. If you are playing a hard rock gig, your snare drum backbeats are probably more important to the band's sound than your ride pattern, so you need to keep the backbeats going while you reach for another stick. On a jazz gig, however, your ride pattern is probably a lot more important than the "comping" you are doing on snare drum, so keep the ride going.

Sometimes silly things happen that you can't do anything about, and that you can't cover up. For example, I was once playing an outdoors show and a strong wind came up, caught the underside of one of my crash cymbals, and blew it over—making a loud crash in the middle of a quiet ballad! All I could do was shake my head and laugh, and the audience laughed too. They saw what happened, and no one blamed me.

The best players don't make faces when they make mistakes, and they don't glare at other band members who make mistakes. The fact is, if you keep your cool, you can often cover up the mistakes in such a way that no one in the audience even knows anything went wrong—as long as you don't signal it by making faces.

When unforeseen things happen, don't lose your cool—instead, be creative. I was once at a club when all the power went out on the stage, silencing the guitar, keyboard, bass, and singer. Without missing a beat (literally!) the drummer went into a drum solo and kept it going for about ten minutes until the power came back on. The crowd loved it!

extras

Back in the 1970s, when bell-bottom pants were in fashion, drummers often got their bass drum beater caught in the front of their pants leg. Some drummers even ripped out the front of their right pants leg when the beater got caught during an especially powerful stroke.

So a lot of drummers got in the habit of rolling up their right pants leg while playing. But then they would forget that they had done that and walk around during breaks with one pants leg rolled up.

EQUIPMENT FAILURES

Broken Sticks

Since sticks do tend to break, you should always keep a supply of them within easy reach. A lot of drummers hang their stick bag on their floor tom so they can easily let a broken stick drop to the floor as they grab a new one. If you break a lot of sticks and you find it awkward to reach across your body when it's your left-hand stick that needs replacement, consider having a stash of sticks on each side of your kit so you can easily grab one with either hand.

Again, try not to let the time feel suffer while you are reaching for another stick. In some cases, you can let one hand do double duty for a measure or two. For example, if you have been playing an eighth-note ride pattern on the hi-hat and hitting backbeats on the snare drum, and you suddenly find yourself with only one drumstick, let that hand play the hi-hat and the snare drum by coming off the hi-hat for the two snare drum notes until you can retrieve another stick. Ideally, you should be able to do this with either hand, but if you can't do it with your left hand, and it was your right stick that broke (or flew away), quickly transfer your left stick to your right hand, keep playing with that, and then reach down to get a new stick with your left hand.

Of course, some breaks are worse than others. If the tip breaks off a stick, you can usually flip the stick over quickly and play with the butt end until the song is over. But be careful about striking a drumhead with the broken end of a stick, as those broken ends can be sharp and pierce a head—and a broken head is a much bigger problem than a broken stick.

Broken Heads

Drumheads have also been known to break in the middle of a song. If it's a tom head, you've probably got other toms you can use instead of that one. You might have to adjust a pattern here or there, but you can usually finish out the song, or even the set, without anyone even knowing that you broke a head.

If you break a snare drum head, that's more serious. Of course, if you have an auxiliary snare drum on your kit, you can just switch to that for the rest of the song. It might not be the ideal sound, but a lot of people won't even know the difference—or they'll think you went to the other drum on purpose to get a different sound. If you need to get through the song and you don't have another snare drum, try hitting rimshots on your smallest tom. That should have enough "pop" to get you through (even if it gives the rest of the song a reggae flavor).

If you break a lot of snare drum heads, you should consider carrying a back-up snare drum with you. I've actually seen drummers pull a drum off a stand and replace it with another one in the middle of a song while still playing bass drum and hi-hat or ride cymbal. (Of course, if you have a roadie, that will make things somewhat easier.) Even if you can't change the drum in the middle of the song, having a spare will get you through the rest of the set so that the band doesn't have to stop while you replace a head.

If you break your bass drum batter head, that's a bigger problem. Of course, if you have two bass drums, you can finish out the song on the good one, although if you broke the head played by your "strong" foot then you'll have to finish out with your "weak" foot. Between songs you might be able to switch drums quickly to get through the rest of the set.

But if you don't have a second bass drum, there's really not much you can do other than slam what would have been the bass drum notes on your lowest floor tom (playing back and forth between the floor tom and snare drum with the same hand), and then stop the show between songs to replace the head. (You ARE carrying extra heads, right?)

Once in the middle of a gig, the lead singer in our band kicked my front bass drum head and split it. (He was trying to dance; it was an ugly sight!) The head was making a "flappy" sound whenever I played the drum, so I couldn't leave it like that, but removing it would have taken several minutes and we had just started a set. So I duct-taped the split and that got me through the rest of the gig.

Pedal Problems

If the beater flies off your bass drum pedal or the spring becomes detached, again, you could try playing the rest of the bass drum notes on your floor tom, and then it's a quick fix to replace the beater or reattach the spring between songs. If the pedal actually breaks, that's a bigger problem. If you have some basic tools with you (screwdrivers, pliers, wrenches), you might be able to fix it, but if something snapped, then you're out of luck. This is why some drummers carry an extra pedal.

Hi-hat pedals can also break, but the most common problem is that the clutch comes loose so that the top hi-hat cymbal comes to rest on the bottom cymbal and you can't open and close it with the pedal. You might be able to stop playing the snare drum for a couple of beats while you tighten the clutch so that the pedal operates again, but you'll probably just have to do without it until you can adjust it between songs. As problems go, that's not as serious as being without a snare drum or bass drum.

BACKUPS

The extra instruments you carry as backups do not have to be as high-quality as your primary instruments. Think of them like the little "donut" spare tires you find in most cars these days. They are just designed to get you through until you can repair or replace the damaged instrument. Many drummers start out on lower-quality equipment and gradually "move up" to more professional gear. Once you do that, instead of selling your old snare drum, bass drum pedal, and hi-hat pedal, consider holding onto them and using them as backups. They'll get you through your gig if something breaks. Still, in order to cover every possible thing that could go wrong with your equipment during a gig, you would have to carry a complete second drumkit with you. That's not very practical. So what *should* you bring?

PREVENTIVE MAINTENANCE

Before we get into that, remember that preventive maintenance is always a good idea. Change your heads regularly, and be on the lookout for a head that is worn so you can change it before it breaks. Check moving parts of pedals such as leather straps, chains, and springs. You can often see where they are worn and about to break. Keep moving parts lubricated, which will minimize wear. Also check the cord or plastic strap that is holding your snares on. If it's worn, replace it.

BACK-UP ESSENTIALS

As for extra parts, for starters be sure to have plenty of drumsticks, as those are most prone to breakage. If you use brushes or mallets, you should have extras of those also. (If you replace such items before they actually break, you can use the old ones as your extras.)

It might be difficult to carry a complete set of extra heads, so just carry the most crucial ones. By all means carry top and bottom snare drum heads. If you have several toms, you might be able to get away without using one of them if a head breaks, but if you only have a couple, at least carry batter heads. Bottom heads don't break very often, and even if they do, you can still play without a bottom tom head (like drummers did in the late 1960s and early '70s). Likewise, for the bass drum; you can get away with just using a batter head, so even though it might be awkward to carry an extra one around, you should do so.

A lot of drum cases have enough room that you can carry an extra head or two in the case. As with sticks, if you change a head before it breaks, that can be the extra head that you carry in your case for emergencies. It might not be the best sounding replacement, but it will get you through the gig.

Figure out what tools you might need to make certain repairs, and keep them in your trap case. Snares and bass drum straps are often held on with screws, so be sure you have a screwdriver. Depending on your equipment, you might need a flat-blade screwdriver as well as a Phillips screwdriver. Pliers can often come in handy for repairs, so you might consider packing regular pliers as well as needle-nose pliers. Of course, don't forget everyone's favorite repair tool: duct tape! It can be used to patch a head or hold something together until it can be properly repaired.

Other items you should carry include extra cymbal felts, snare cord, tension lugs, wing nuts, bass drum strap, and—above all—a drum key. And although this isn't a "repair" item, having one has saved me on many occasions: a small piece of carpet. There is nothing worse than arriving at a gig and finding out you have to set your drums on a slick linoleum floor. Your bass drum will be scooting forward every time you hit it, and the hi-hat pedal will tend to slide, too. So you need a piece of carpeting just big enough to cover the area where your bass drum and hi-hat are positioned. It can be very thin carpeting; mine is so thin I can fold it in quarters and carry it in my bass drum case. Most of the time I don't need it, but when I do, I am very glad I have it. Carpet stores often have "remnants" that are very inexpensive.

CHAPTER 27
CHAPTER 27
OPPORTUNITIES

What's Ahead:
- Versatility
- Drumming and singing
- Finding a gig
- Recording
- Getting replaced

Let's face it: there are not as many opportunities to play drums in public as there used to be. DJs are now taking a lot of the work that used to go to bands, and some live bands now use programmed drum machines instead of real drummers. Of course, drummers have never gotten as many gigs as people who can play, say, solo piano, or who can strum a guitar and sing. Not too many people (if any) are going to hire a solo drummer. Just about all of our work comes from playing in a band.

VERSATILITY

The drummers who work the most are the ones who are versatile. They can play at least a couple of different styles, which means that they might do a rock gig one night and a country gig another night. If they are especially versatile, they can land a gig with a wedding band or dance band that does a variety of styles. For such gigs you don't have to be an absolute master of all styles, just be able to play basic rock, jazz, Latin, funk, and country feels.

Good variety bands can still get a fair share of work at weddings, parties, dances, and "society" events that cater to a slightly older crowd that is more used to live music than to DJs. So if you want to play in such a group, do your homework and learn basic jazz "standards"; rock tunes from the 1950s, '60s, and '70s; and basic Latin and dance beats. Also be sure to learn how to play "novelty" numbers like the "Duck Dance" (also known as the "Chicken Dance") and the "Hokey Pokey." Bands are often hired for Bar Mitzvahs as well, so learn "Hava Nagila."

DRUMMING AND SINGING

In addition to being versatile in terms of knowing a lot of styles, you can also increase your "hirability" by being able to sing. You don't necessarily have to sing lead vocals, but if you can harmonize on songs, then that will give you an advantage over a drummer who only plays drums. (Of course, if you can do a lead vocal or two to give the singer a rest now and then, so much the better.)

Singing from behind the drums used to be a major hassle because of microphone placement. Drummers can't have mic stands set up right in front of them the way guitar players can, so they have to use boom stands and try to arrange everything in such a way that the stand won't interfere with the arm movements a drummer makes. But with the invention of headset mics, that problem has been eliminated. So if you want to promote yourself as a singing drummer, you should acquire your own headset mic.

You also need to practice playing and singing at the same time. If you've never tried it before, you may be surprised at how difficult it can be to keep a drumset beat going while you are singing lyrics that have their own rhythm pattern. Many drummers say it's like coordinating a fifth limb! But however awkward it might feel at first, most drummers get the hang of it pretty quickly. And playing drums to your own singing can help you learn a lot about what kind of support a singer needs from a drummer. For example, you'll naturally save your fills for the spots between phrases when you are not singing, and that's when you should play your fills when someone else is singing, too.

FINDING A GIG

Some cities have active club scenes with live music. If you are hoping to play in some of those clubs, you should visit them regularly. Get familiar with the type of music that is played in specific clubs, and get to know the musicians who play there. Get the word out that you are interested in joining a band that plays a similar style of music. The musicians in one band may very well know of other musicians who are forming a band and are looking for a drummer.

If you can't find a band to join, consider starting your own. Again, talk to musicians who are already playing. Let them know you are putting a group together and ask them if they know any musicians looking for a band to join.

Rock bands are usually made up of a specific group of musicians, but jazz musicians often like to play in different combinations. So if you are interested in jazz, again, go to jazz clubs and get to know the players. Let people know that you play jazz and that you are available for jam sessions. If you have a place large enough for several musicians to play in, invite players you like to jam with you. Once you start playing with a few people, word will get around and, if you can play, people will probably start calling you for gigs.

Some clubs let musicians sit in during late-night sets. If there is such a situation in your town, take advantage of it. The way to get hired is to let as many people as possible hear you play, and sitting in is a great way to promote yourself.

If a local university has a music program, see if there are any opportunities there. The school might sponsor a community jazz band that you could play in. That's a great way to meet other players.

Hanging out in music stores can also help you find people to play with. The people who work in stores always know a lot of musicians, and they often know of people who are looking for a new band member. Of course, the best way to become friends with people who work at music stores is to give them your business. Do NOT spend hours in a local shop trying out different instruments and getting advice from the salesclerks, and then make all your purchases online. If you are going to take advantage of the services a local shop provides, then give that shop your business. And remember that the salespeople in local music shops can do a lot to help you find other musicians to play with.

Some music stores have bulletin boards on which musicians can post notices. You might find a notice from a band looking for a drummer, and you can also post your own "Drummer Looking For Work" notice. Have some business cards printed up. Your card should include your name, instrument, phone number, and e-mail address, and you should also list the style or styles of music you play.

RECORDING

Quite honestly, there isn't as much recording work for drummers as there used to be. Years ago, a lot of drummers were able to break into recording by doing "demo" sessions for songwriters, but most songwriters now make their own demos with computer programs and/or synthesizers and drum machines.

These days, most drummers first get into studios if they are members of bands who have a record deal or who go into the studio to make their own demos or CDs. If the studio engineer is impressed with your playing, he might recommend you to someone who needs a drummer for a session. And even if he doesn't approach you, before you leave the session, you should give him your business card and tell him you'd be interested in doing some studio work. Besides looking for good players, producers, artists, and engineers look for musicians who are cooperative. Studio time is expensive, so they need a drummer who can come up with the right part quickly and take direction.

That direction usually comes from the engineer. Even if your band has booked the session, remember that this is the engineer's turf. He knows his room and he probably has a good idea of where the drums should be and how they should be miked. When you first go in, ask him where he would like you to set up. There might already be a miked-up drumset in the studio, and if you can use that, it will save everyone time and effort.

If, when you hear the first playback, there is something you aren't happy about, by all means bring it to the engineer's attention—with courtesy and respect. If you have already shown yourself to be cooperative, the engineer will be more likely to change something to fit your particular preferences. (And the best engineers will constantly ask *you* if you are happy and if there is anything you would like changed.) The engineer can be your best friend in the studio, or your worst enemy. Do everything you can to make this person your friend.

GETTING REPLACED

One of the worst nightmares for many drummers is the day they finally get to go into the studio with their band, and the record-company producer informs them that a professional studio musician is going to do the drumming. If that should happen, as difficult as it might be, accept the situation and stay in the studio to see how it's done. You can learn a tremendous amount by sitting next to an accomplished studio musician and observing—and listening!—to what he or she does.

Do NOT start feeling sorry for yourself, thinking that you are the only person this has ever happened to. Most of today's great studio drummers got replaced in the studio early in their careers. When Kenny Aronoff first went in the studio with John Mellencamp, he was told that a studio drummer was going to do the tracks. Kenny stayed, and on one song he ended up playing vibes. But mostly he listened and learned. Now he's one of the busiest studio drummers in the business.

The same thing happened to Andy Newmark when Carly Simon was doing her third album. Andy had played on her second album, which included the hit "Anticipation." But the record company wanted the third album to be a real smash, so they brought in studio musicians for the songs that were deemed likely to be singles. Andy stayed in the studio and watched Jim Gordon record the tracks. "I realized how much space there was in his playing," Newmark said. "I learned more from watching him than I would have learned from playing those songs myself."

Likewise, Jim Keltner was replaced by Gordon in the studio early in his career. But, like Aronoff and Newmark, he viewed the situation as a learning situation, and went on to become an in-demand studio drummer himself.

Studio drumming is very different than live drumming, and it takes some practice. So if you ultimately hope to be a studio drummer, you need to work on those skills. Set up your own home studio so you can hear yourself. (You might be surprised to find that you don't sound as good as you thought you did.) Invite other musicians over to play with you, and record it. Get used to playing with a click track. Experiment with miking. When you finally get your chance, be as prepared as possible. But if you are asked to step aside so an experienced studio drummer can play, take advantage of the opportunity to learn from it.

Equipment

CHAPTER 28
HISTORY OF THE DRUMSET

> **What's Ahead:**
> - Origins
> - Early drumsets
> - Early jazz drumkits
> - R&B and rock 'n' roll kits
> - Electronic kits
> - Modern drumsets

ORIGINS

The modern drumset can be said to have originated with the invention of the bass drum pedal, which first appeared in the 1890s, but didn't achieve widespread popularity until perfected by the Ludwig Drum Co. in 1909. The bass drum pedal allowed a single performer sitting on a stool to play both snare drum and bass drum. One could argue that the invention of the bass drum pedal put half the drummers out of work, as one person could now do the work of two!

Gradually, other drums, cymbals, percussion instruments, and sound effects were added. The individual components were borrowed from a variety of cultures. The snare drum and bass drum were of the style used by European military and concert bands. The original tom-toms used with drumsets were Chinese drums with tacked-on heads. The cymbals were of Turkish and Chinese origin and were the type used in military bands, concert bands, and orchestras. These cymbals, which were generally 10 to 15 inches in diameter, were mounted on stands and used for short crashes and accents. Combining all of these instruments into a single drumset is considered a U.S. innovation.

EARLY DRUMSETS

Early drumsets were often called "trapkits" or "traps." Today, not everyone agrees as to the origin of the term. Many contend that the term "traps" originated around the 1920s as a result of the various woodblocks, cowbells, ratchets, temple blocks, and sound-effects devices that adorned the drumkits of vaudeville, theater, and dance band drummers, which were often referred to as "trappings." Other explanations include the fact that the drumset was considered a conTRAPtion, or that the bass drum and early hi-hat pedals resembled bear traps.

In the early 1920s, a device called the "snow-shoe" or the "Charleston pedal" appeared, consisting of two cymbals mounted on hinged boards that could be clapped together with the foot. Around 1925 a drummer named Vic Berton developed the low-boy or "sock cymbals," which resembled the modern hi-hat except that the cymbals were only about 15 inches above the floor. Soon afterwards, the tube that extended between the cymbals and the pedal was elongated so that the cymbals were higher, allowing them to be played with sticks, and the low-boy became the hi-hat.

Theater drummers in the early part of the 20th century used drumsets along with timpani, xylophones, and other orchestral percussion instruments, functioning as one-person percussion sections. But it was the Dixieland and early jazz band drummers who developed the performance style that evolved into modern drumset playing.

EARLY JAZZ DRUMKITS

At first, jazz drumset players such as Baby Dodds and Chick Webb did most of their accompaniment playing on just a snare drum and bass drum, much in the style of military drummers, using a lot of rolls and rudimental figures. By the time of the Swing era, such drummers as Jo Jones, Gene Krupa, and Buddy Rich were playing "time" on a ride cymbal or hi-hat, maintaining a steady pulse on the bass drum and using the snare drum to reinforce accents in ensemble riffs or in a comping style. Tom-toms were used primarily in conjunction with the snare drum for fills and solos, but sometimes drummers would perform primarily on tom-toms to produce what was called a "jungle" sound.

Swing drummers also pioneered the use of wire brushes on the snare drum, which provided a soft, legato sound that was especially effective on ballads. By this time, few drummers were using the small percussion instruments and sound effects that had previously been included as part of the drumset, and most drumsets consisted entirely of drums and cymbals. A typical drumset of the period had a 26-inch diameter bass drum, a snare drum, one tom-tom mounted over the bass drum, a floor tom, a pair of hi-hat cymbals, a ride cymbal, and two or three crash cymbals.

Bebop drummers of the 1940s and '50s, such Kenny Clarke, Max Roach, Art Blakey, Philly Joe Jones, Roy Haynes, and Elvin Jones, put more emphasis on the ride cymbal as the primary timekeeper, maintained pedal hi-hat on the second and fourth beats of the bar ("backbeats"), and de-emphasized the bass drum, using it for occasional loud accents ("dropping bombs") rather than to maintain a constant pulse. Because bebop was typically played by groups with three to seven players, it was not necessary for the drummer to hold the band together with a loud bass drum pulse, as was the case with the big band drummers of the Swing era. Also, because bebop was not considered dance music, drummers were freer to use the bass drum for syncopated accents rather than for maintaining a dance beat. Some bebop drummers did, however, often maintain a soft quarter-note pulse on the bass drum, a technique often referred to as "feathering" the drum. The typical bebop drumset had the same configuration as the drumsets used by big band drummers, but the sizes of the drums tended to be smaller, especially the bass drums, with 18-inch and 20-inch diameter bass drums becoming common.

As jazz drummers of the 1940s began using larger cymbals to maintain a continuous time-keeping pattern, cymbals began to be classified as rides or crashes, and different weights were developed ranging from "paper thin" to heavy, in order to accommodate an increasing demand for a variety of cymbal sounds. Some modern drumsets have more cymbals than drums, and cymbals have evolved from mere sound effects to crucial elements in a drummer's performance, with the ride cymbal and hi-hat considered equal in importance to the snare drum and bass drum for basic timekeeping.

R&B AND ROCK 'N' ROLL KITS

In the early 1950s, a style of music called rhythm and blues (R&B) developed, which combined bebop and blues with a steady dance beat. The shuffle became the dominant rhythm pattern, often played simultaneously on the snare drum and ride cymbal with accented backbeats.

When rock 'n' roll developed in the 1950s, drummers started putting emphasis on the snare drum and bass drum again, using them to play repetitive patterns ("beats" or "grooves") that emphasized backbeats on the snare drum. Because of the volume of rock 'n' roll, drummers preferred larger drums than those used by bebop drummers, and 22-inch bass drums became standard.

As late as the mid-1960s, such rock drummers as Ringo Starr (with the Beatles) and Charlie Watts (with the Rolling Stones) were still using the same basic configuration of drums and cymbals that had been standardized by bebop drummers (bass drum, snare drum, mounted tom-tom, floor tom, ride cymbal, hi-hat, and one or two crash cymbals.) But in the mid-1960s many drummers added a second tom-tom mounted on their bass drums, and from the late 1960s on, some rock 'n' roll drummers, such as Ginger Baker (Cream), Keith Moon (The Who) and Neil Peart (Rush), used two bass drums (pioneered by jazz drummer Louis Bellson in 1938), as many as eight tom-toms, and a wide variety of cymbals.

Some drummers added other percussion instruments, such as Carl Palmer's use of large gongs with Emerson, Lake and Palmer; John Bonham's use of timpani with Led Zeppelin; and Peart's use of tubular chimes with Rush. Such instruments were only used as special effects, however. The rock influence also affected the setups of jazz drummers such as Tony Williams (Lifetime) and Billy Cobham (Mahavishnu Orchestra), whose drumsets resembled the larger kits used by rock drummers.

ELECTRONIC KITS

In the 1980s, electronic drumsets appeared, pioneered by Simmons. Such drummers as Terry Bozzio (with Missing Persons) and Bill Bruford (with King Crimson and Earthworks) briefly used all-electronic kits (although sometimes with acoustic cymbals), but despite predictions that electronic kits would make acoustic drumsets obsolete, most drummers stayed with acoustic kits, although some would add one or more electronic pads as alternate sound sources.

MODERN DRUMSETS

By the 1990s, it was difficult to designate any particular configuration of drums and cymbals as "standard." Some drummers stayed with "classic" four-piece and five-piece kits with just a few cymbals, other drummers used enormous kits featuring multiple toms, cymbals, and bass drums, as well as a variety of electronic devices and ethnic percussion instruments. And, of course, you could find just about anything in between those extremes.

In many respects, the drumset has come full-circle. In the 1920s and '30s, big band and theater drummers used a wide variety of drums, cymbals, and sound effects to add as much color as possible to the music. Then, for several decades, many different styles of music were all played on the same basic drum-and-cymbals setups. Now, many drummers are again incorporating a wide variety of instruments into their setups, adapting their drumkits to the varied demands of modern music.

CHAPTER 29
TYPES AND SIZES OF DRUMSETS

> **What's Ahead:**
> - Jazz
> - Classic rock and country
> - Hard rock, metal, and fusion
> - Progressive rock

As you've probably noticed from seeing drummers on TV, in videos, and in live performance, no two drumsets seem to be exactly the same. Drumkits can be assembled from a wide variety of drum and cymbal models; players can customize their kits to fit their own playing styles.

Nevertheless, there are some elements common to all drumsets. If there is a single configuration that can be considered "basic," it is a five-piece set consisting of bass drum, snare drum, two mounted (or "rack") tom-toms, and floor tom. Such kits will generally also include a ride cymbal, a crash cymbal, and a hi-hat assembly.

From there, you can add or subtract instruments depending on the needs of the music you are playing. Following is a brief guide to matching a drumset to a style of music. But these are very general suggestions. Note that you can find almost any drumset configuration in just about any genre of music. The following ideas are just to get you started.

JAZZ

Many traditional jazz drummers like to use what is considered a traditional jazz kit: a bass drum, a snare drum, one mounted tom, and one floor tom. For acoustic jazz gigs, drummers often prefer smaller drum sizes: an 18" or 20" bass drum, an 8 × 12 rack tom, a 14 × 14 floor tom, and a 4 × 14 snare drum. Many jazz drummers prefer wood-shell snare drums to metal drums.

A lot of jazz drummers will tell you that the single most important part of their kit is the ride cymbal. In fact, many jazz drummers use two ride cymbals so they can change the color from tune to tune. Generally, one of the rides will be a 20" model. The other might be an 18" or a 22". One of them might also have rivets. The crash cymbal is usually 16" or 18", and the hi-hats are generally 14" or 13".

Jazz drummers often prefer cymbals modeled after the K Zildjians that were originally made in Istanbul ("old Ks"). The Avedis Zildjian company markets these under the original name K Zildjian, and similar models include Sabian HH (Hand Hammered) cymbals, Paiste Traditionals, and cymbals made by Bosphorus and Istanbul. Such cymbals have a darker sound and what are sometimes referred to as "trashy" overtones (but to those who love the sound, "trashy" is a compliment).

CLASSIC ROCK AND COUNTRY

Many classic rock and country drummers also use four-piece drumkits, but the sizes are larger than those preferred by jazz drummers: a 22" bass drum, 5 × 14 snare drum, 9 × 13 rack tom, and a 16 × 16 floor tom. Some classic rock drummers expand to a five-piece kit with the addition of an 8 × 12 rack tom.

A standard cymbal setup for such a kit is a 20" ride cymbal, 16" and 18" crash cymbals, and 14" hi-hats. Most rock drummers prefer brighter cymbals such as Sabian AAs, A Zildjians, or Paiste 2002s.

HARD ROCK, METAL, AND FUSION

Some hard rock, metal, and fusion drummers also use five-piece kits, but with "power size" drums with greater depth than standard drums: a standard bass drum might be 14×22, whereas a power bass drum would be 16×22.

But many hard rock drummers go for two bass drums, and in most cases, they will also have additional toms, with a standard setup including 8", 10", 12", and 14" rack toms (in power depths), and 16" and 18" floor toms.

Such kits will generally include a variety of crash cymbals, including a China cymbal or two. The cymbals will often be extra heavy, such as Zildjian's Z series, Sabain's AA Metal-X series, Paiste's Rude series, or Meinl's Mb20 series.

PROGRESSIVE ROCK

It's difficult to designate a typical setup for progressive rock, as the drumkits tend to be as varied as the music. Suffice it to say that prog rock drummers tend to use large setups with a wide variety of sonic possibilities, including acoustic drums and cymbals, electronics, sound effects, and world percussion instruments. Neil Peart of Rush was known for his extravagant drumset which, besides many drums and cymbals, included a variety of orchestral and Latin percussion instruments. For a photo of Peart's kit, see Section 10, "Who's Who."

CHAPTER 30
CHAPTER 30
BRANDS AND MODELS

What's Ahead:
- Make and model "levels"
- Drum shell types
- Leading drumset manufacturers
- Cymbal makers

MAKE AND MODEL "LEVELS"

There are a lot of drums out there. In addition to all of the different manufacturers, each company offers a variety of models. How do you figure out, then, which drums to buy?

Price is often a good starting point. Figure out what you can afford and then see what is available in that price range. The price ranges discussed below are based on "list" prices: the prices the manufacturers suggest that their kits should be sold for. But many music stores sell instruments at discount prices, so you might, for example, find a good semi-pro kit for under $1,000.

The guidelines below are based on a standard five-piece drumset with bass drum, snare drum, two rack toms, and floor tom. Note that drumset prices typically do not include cymbals.

So, with that in mind, if a drumset's list price is under $1,000, you are generally looking at an "entry level" kit. The closer you get to $1,000, the better the kit will usually be, and the more likely that it is made by one of the leading drum manufacturers. The lower the price, the more likely that the kit is made in Taiwan by a company that puts a variety of different names on their drums.

Entry-level

Entry-level kits tend to be made from mahogany or basswood, the hardware is usually not very sturdy, and the drumheads are often substandard. Sometimes, just replacing the heads with quality heads can improve the sound tremendously.

Entry-level kits are designed to learn on. Generally, if you set them up in your house and leave them there, they can last a long time. One of the main problems with entry-level kits is that if you start moving them around a lot, they are more easily damaged than higher-quality kits.

Semi-professional

Once you get into kits with list prices between about $1,000 and $1,500, you are in the semi-pro range. It's usually worth it to save your money and go for a semi-pro kit rather than an entry-level kit, because the quality is generally a lot higher. Many drummers who do weekend gigs use semi-pro kits. They will generally be made from better wood, have sturdier hardware, have better looking finishes, and be fitted with quality drumheads.

Professional

To get into the truly professional range, you will probably be spending over $2,000. You will be getting premium woods, often with natural finishes (as opposed to a covering over the shell), and the hardware will be strong and functional. Note that in some cases, a lot of the extra money might be going more into the finish than into the materials or workmanship, so compare those features carefully between the pro and semi-pro models in a given line.

DRUM SHELL TYPES

Once you've settled on the price range you can afford, you might want to compare the shells in the different kits available in that range. Maple is the most widely used wood for drum shells. It produces a rich sound across the middle of the frequency range, so the drums have a good, all-purpose sound. Birch shells tend to have a little better high-frequency response. Mahogany shells favor the low end. Some drummers like their "warmth," while others think that mahogany shells sound "muddy."

Most drums are made from several layers of wood, called *plies*. Inexpensive drums might have maple or mahogany outer layers, but with some sort of cheap "filler" wood in between. Some high-end drums might have combinations of maple and birch plies. Generally, the more plies a drum has, the thicker the shell. But, for example, three thick plies could result in a thicker shell than six thin plies, so when ascertaining shell thickness, don't just count the plies.

The thicker the shell, the less it will vibrate, and that will affect the tone and the projection. Thin shells have a lot of resonance and produce a deep, rich tone. They are often favored by jazz drummers. Medium-thick shells are a little brighter sounding and project better. They are best for all-purpose use. Thick shells have the most projection, and are favored by heavy rock drummers for their volume and strength.

When it comes to snare drums, another option is a metal shell. Essentially, metal-shell snare drums are brighter sounding than wood-shell snare drums. But just as there are different woods used in drums, so too are there different metals. Brass drums often sound a bit warmer than chrome or nickel drums, for example.

Remember that drums are acoustic instruments. Unlike an electric guitar, which can be made to sound almost like any other electric guitar by turning a few knobs or stomping on a pedal or two, there isn't much you can do to change the basic characteristics of a drum sound, apart from using different heads and tunings. That's why it's best to try drums out before you buy them. Find a music shop that has an assortment of kits on display and find out for yourself which sounds the best to you.

LEADING DRUMSET MANUFACTURERS

The following is a brief guide to the top drum and cymbal manufacturers. In addition, there are various specialty and custom drum companies, but these are the ones you are most likely to encounter in typical music stores and drum shops.

Drum Workshop (DW)

DW is an American manufacturer of professional drums, pedals, and hardware. The company is especially known for its superb craftsmanship, exotic finishes, and chain-drive bass drum pedals. With its many options for sizes, wood types, and finishes, DW is essentially a custom shop that provides drummers the opportunity to design their own setups.

www.dwdrums.com

Gretsch

Gretsch is a legendary American drum maker that features a full range of professional, semi-pro, and entry-level drumkits. The company is especially noted for its professional maple-shell drums and beautiful wood finishes. Models include USA Maple and USA Custom (pro), Catalina Birch (semi-pro), and Blackhawk and Catalina Club (entry level).

www.gretschdrums.com

Ludwig

Ludwig is another legendary American drum maker, one that originally perfected the bass drum pedal and now offers a full range of professional, semi-pro, and entry-level drumkits. The company is especially known for its Speed King bass drum pedal and Supraphonic snare drum. Drumset models include Classic Maple (pro), Classic Birch (semi-pro), and Accent (entry level).

www.Ludwig-drums.com

Mapex

This company is a manufacturer of a full range of drumsets for professionals as well as beginners. Series include Saturn, Orion, and Pro M (pro), VX (semi-pro), and Q Series (entry level).

www.mapexdrums.com

Pacific Drums and Percussion

This is a subsidiary of Drum Workshop that specializes in affordable drumsets and hardware.

www.pacificdrums.com

Pearl

Pearl is a manufacturer of a full range of drumsets, marching drums, and concert drums, with sets geared for professionals as well as beginners. The company is especially known for its Export series kits, which combine high quality with an affordable price. Other series include Reference (pro, 20-ply shells combining birch and maple), Masterworks (pro, custom shells), Session (semi-pro), and Forum (entry level).

www.pearldrum.com

Premier

Premier is a British manufacturer of drums and percussion instruments. Models include the Premier Series (pro, available with maple or birch shells), Cabria (semi-pro), and Olympic (entry level).

www.premier-percussion.com

Sonor

Sonor is a German manufacturer of very high-quality drumsets. The company is best known for its high-end drumkits (Designer, Delite, S Class Pro), but also makes more affordable sets (Force 2005, Force 505).

www.sonor-world.com

Tama

This company is a manufacturer of a wide range of drumsets, including the Starclassic and Superstar (pro), Swingstar (semi-pro), and Stagestar (entry level) series. Tama is especially known for its heavy-duty products such as the Iron Cobra bass drum pedal, geared for hard rock drummers.

www.tama.com

Taye

Taye makes several drumset configurations in a variety of premium woods, with many custom features.

www.tayedrums.com

Yamaha

This Japanese company makes a huge assortment of drums, hardware, and accessories for every level of player, and at a variety of price ranges. The company is especially well-known for its birch-shell drums. Series include Recording Custom and Maple Custom (pro), Advantage (semi-pro), and Rydeen (entry level).

www.yamahadrums.com

CYMBAL MAKERS

Despite all of the different models of cymbals that exist, there are two basic types, often referred to as "cast" and "sheet metal" (or "non-cast") cymbals. Actually, all cymbals are cast in one way or another, but the difference is that in the Turkish style, each cymbal has its own casting that is then rolled out into a circular shape. In the Swiss and German style, the cymbal metal is cast into large sheets, and then individual cymbals are stamped out of those sheets.

Is one method better than the other? No. But each has its own characteristics. Fans of the Swiss/German method claim that those cymbals are more consistent; for example, every 20" medium ride in a certain model will sound exactly the same. Fans of "cast" cymbals counter that the individual castings create a unique tonal personality for each cymbal.

Top-line Zildjian, Sabian, Bosphorus, and Istanbul cymbals are cast. Paiste and Meinl cymbals are non-cast, as are lower-priced Zildjians and Sabians.

Quality cymbals are made of bronze, which is a combination of copper and tin. Most cymbals are made of either B20 (80% copper, 20% tin) or B8 (92% copper, 8% tin) bronze. In general, the professional-line Sabian, Zildjian, Istanbul, Bosphorus, and some Paiste series are made of B20, while most Paiste cymbals, Meinl, and lower-price Zildjians and Sabians are made from B8.

Very inexpensive cymbals are usually made of brass, which is very yellowish in color, or nickel-silver. (There is no silver in the metal, however; the name refers to the silverish color.)

Now that you know all of that, should you care? Well, you probably want to stay away from bronze or nickel-silver cymbals, but when deciding between B20 and B8 cymbals, use your ears, not a metallurgic formula. Some people prefer one over the other; some people have both in their setups to get a wide variety of sounds.

Most cymbals are lathed and hammered. With some cymbals, the lathing is much more obvious. That's the process that results in the circular patterns that some people call "tonal grooves." With other cymbals, the hammering is more obvious because of the "dents" in the body of the cymbal. All cymbals are hammered to some extent, but some cymbals are not lathed. Again, don't buy a cymbal because of the manufacturing process. Different hammering and lathing techniques are used to create different styles of cymbals, so use your ears.

Some cymbals are said to be "hand hammered." In some cases, each cymbal is actually hammered by hand. But in a lot of cases, that term is just used to refer to a cymbal that has the characteristics of "old style" cymbals as opposed to more modern models, and many "hand hammered" cymbals are actually hammered by machines.

However romantic the idea of true hand hammering might sound, machine hammering is much more consistent. If a cymbal really is hammered by hand, you'll want to hear it before you buy it.

In general, the "smoother" cymbals in which the lathing is more obvious are the more "mainstream" cymbals such as most Paistes and Meinls, Sabian AAs, and A Zildjians. The cymbals with more obvious hammering tend to be darker (and sometimes "trashy"), such as Sabian HH, K Zildjian, Bosphorus, and Istanbul cymbals.

The following are the leading cymbal companies whose products you are most likely to encounter:

Bosphorus

This Istanbul company specializes in Turkish-style, hand-hammered cast cymbals.

www.bosphoruscymbals.com

Istanbul

This Turkish company specializes in "traditional" hand-hammered cymbals.

www.istanbulcymbals.com

Meinl

This German company offers cymbals for a variety of applications in a wide range of prices.

www.meinlcymbals.com

Paiste

This Swiss company manufactures a full range of cymbals including Traditional, Signature, Giant Beat, 2002, Rude, Innovations, Noise Works, and other series in a wide range of prices.

www.paiste.com

Sabian

This Canadian company features a full range of cymbals in a variety of styles and price ranges, including AA, Hand Hammered, HHX, B8 Pro, and others.

www.sabian.com

Zildjian

This American company manufactures a complete selection of cymbals, including A Zildjian, K Zildjian, Z series, K Custom, K Constantinople, and others, covering a wide range of styles and prices.

www.zildjian.com

Old Ks

When the descendents of Avedis Zildjian left Turkey to start the Avedis Zildjian Company in America, the descendents of Kerope Zildjian stayed in their native country, making cymbals under the name K Zildjian. The American Zildjians pioneered new manufacturing methods, designing machines that could do the lathing and hammering, thus bringing more consistency to the cymbals. Meanwhile, K Zildjian cymbals continued to be made by "traditional" techniques.

From about the 1940s into the mid-1970s, K Zildjian cymbals were favored by many jazz drummers for their dark, "trashy" sound. K Zildjians were imported by the Gretsch drum company, whose drums were also favored by jazz drummers, so it was typical to see players such as Art Blakey, Max Roach, Elvin Jones, Mel Lewis, and Philly Joe Jones playing Gretsch drums and K Zildjian cymbals.

In the late 1970s, the Avedis Zildjian company purchased all rights to the name K Zildjian and began manufacturing their own line of K Zildjians in their Canadian factory, under the supervision of Gabe Zilcan, a great-grandson of Kerope Zildjian. Soon after, brothers Armand and Robert Zildjian parted ways, with Armand retaining the Avedis Zildjian company and Robert acquiring the Canadian factory, which he renamed Sabian (for his children, SAlly, BIlly, and ANdy). The Ks that had been made in Canada were renamed HH (Hand Hammered), and the Avedis Zildjian company began making yet another line of K's in the U.S.

The K Zildjians that were originally made in Turkey started being referred to as "old K's." If you found a good "old K," you were in luck. But one of the things about old K's was their inconsistency, due to the ancient manufacturing methods. Mel Lewis told me that he once went through a shipment of over a hundred K's at the Gretsch factory and didn't find a single one he liked. Granted, Mel had very specific tastes, but a 20" medium ride, say, could range from fairly thin to fairly thick. The bell might be very deep or very shallow (or anything in between), and the hole in the bell might not be centered. One really had to choose an old K carefully.

By contrast, the American K Zildjians and the Sabian HH cymbals were much more consistent. But for a long time most people felt that the modern versions were somewhere in between old K's and modern A Zildjians. Ultimately, Zildjian introduced the Constantinople series of K Zildjians, which are much more in the tradition of old K's. Meanwhile, companies such as Bosphorus and Istanbul are specializing in cymbals made the "traditional" Turkish way.

But to a lot of people, there is still something about a genuine "old K." If you find a good one, you've really got something.

CHAPTER 31

THRONES

What's Ahead:

- Comfort and function
- Seat shapes
- Throne height
- Back support

I've seen drummers spend thousands of dollars on state-of-the-art drums and cymbals, then sit on a cheap throne, a folding chair, or their trap case. But in fact, your drum throne can be crucial to your technique as well as to your health!

COMFORT AND FUNCTION

First of all, you want a throne that is comfortable. You are going to be spending a *lot* of time sitting there, and you owe it to yourself to be as comfy as possible so you can concentrate on playing the music without being distracted by a sore rear-end (or back).

But by "comfortable," I don't mean you should buy the throne with the biggest, softest cushioned seat you can find. If the seat is too large and you sink down into it too far, it can restrict your leg movements.

So find a throne that is reasonably soft, but that is also firm enough to support you. And match the size of the seat to the part of your body that is going to be sitting there. Don't get a bigger seat than you need. While playing, you only want the drum seat to be under your buttocks; it should not also be supporting any part of your upper leg. That can restrict your freedom of movement. If you have a large drum seat and a small backside, you can always sit toward the front of the seat while playing.

Also make sure that the throne you select is solid and stable. Even if you are small in stature and/or do not weigh very much, the movements you make as you are playing with all four limbs can put a lot of stress on your throne. So get one that has firm legs (double-braced legs are always a good idea on thrones) and on which the legs extend out far enough that you won't topple over in the middle of a hot, energetic drum solo.

SEAT SHAPES

Drum seats come in several shapes. The majority of models are round, but there are also "saddle" seats that are shaped like large bicycle seats, and there are even a few square seats on the market. Deciding which one is best is totally your decision, based on your own body shape and size. Choose the one that is most comfortable and allows you the most freedom of movement.

THRONE HEIGHT

When setting up the throne, you should also match its height to your body—especially your legs. If you have long legs, you need to set it higher; if you have short legs, the throne can be lower. When you are trying to determine the proper height, sit on the throne with your feet on the bass drum and hi-hat pedals (or on two bass drum pedals, or a double bass pedal, or whatever combination of pedals you use most often).

With your feet resting on the pedals (and with the heels of your shoes resting on the pedals as well), your upper legs should be angled down very slightly. Now raise your heels however high you raise them when you are playing with a toe-technique. If your upper legs end up parallel to the floor, or especially if your knees are pointing up, you need to raise your seat slightly. You always want your upper leg to be aimed downward at least a little bit. This gives you the most power and control so that all of your energy goes into playing, not into raising your legs up in the air so that you can get enough momentum for your downstroke. It also helps ensure good blood circulation to your lower legs, ankles, and feet.

Once you have your throne set at the optimum height for your foot technique, adjust the rest of your kit to fit the height at which you are now sitting. Start with the instruments you play the most, which will probably be the snare drum, hi-hat, and ride cymbal. Don't have them so low that you have to slouch over to hit them—that will ultimately cause lower-back problems. Don't have them so high that you have to hold your arms up in the air to play them. Your upper arm should be hanging straight down when playing the main parts of your kit.

Now adjust the other drums and cymbals on your kit. Do your best to adjust the instruments you play most often so that you don't have to use too much extra arm movement to get to them. If you have a huge kit, you might have to stretch a little to get to a few of the cymbals and toms, but remember that having to stretch too far not only strains your muscles, it can also affect your timing, and what good are we drummers without good time?

BACK SUPPORT

You might consider a throne that has a backrest. Such a throne can help you sit up straighter, thus preventing back pain. Even if you want to lean forward a bit when you are actually playing (which is usually a good idea), being able to sit back and relax between songs can do a lot to ease the strain on your back muscles.

Care and Maintenance

CHAPTER 32

DRUMHEADS AND TUNING

What's Ahead:
* Drumhead types
* Tuning
* Acoustics

I've known of drummers spending thousands of dollars on a new drumset because their old drumset sounds "dead" to them and they wanted a fuller, brighter sound. Granted, some drums have more resonance than others, but I've seen many cases in which the problem isn't the drums, it's the drumheads. The heads might be so old and battered that they have lost all of their resonance. Or, they may not be tuned properly, and so there is no clear tone being produced for the shell to amplify.

Even if the heads are new and tuned properly, they might be the wrong types of heads for the sound you want. So before we discuss tuning, let's look at the most common types of drumheads.

DRUMHEAD TYPES

Single-ply Heads

Single-ply heads—heads that are made from a single layer of plastic (usually Mylar)—are used on the majority of drums and are considered the most "general purpose." But not all single-ply heads are created equal. They can be of different thicknesses (thin, medium, or heavy), and can be clear or coated.

Thin heads are the most responsive and also favor higher tuning ranges. But they are also the easiest to break. Medium heads have a good balance between responsiveness, strength, and tuning range. Thick heads are not quite as responsive, favor a lower tuning range, and are the strongest of the single-ply heads.

Clear heads generally have more tone. A coating muffles the sound somewhat, but that can be desirable on a batter head, because usually you want to get your attack from the batter head and most of your tone and pitch from the "resonant" head (the bottom head of a tom or the front head of a bass drum). Therefore, many drummers use a coated head on top and a clear head on the bottom.

For snare drum heads, a coating helps give the drier sound that most people want from a snare drum, and the coating also provides the friction needed for brush playing.

Double-ply Heads

Double-ply (or two-ply) heads are stronger than single-ply heads, and they also tend to be drier sounding because the two plies muffle each other somewhat. Double-ply heads are generally used only as batter heads. You don't need the extra strength on your bottom heads, since you are not hitting them, and you'll want more resonance on the bottom than a typical two-ply head provides.

Specialty Heads

Dotted Heads

Some heads have "dots" in the middle: an extra layer of mylar that is glued to the head to add strength in the center and muffle a few of the extra overtones. Like double-ply models, these are best for batter heads.

Pinstripe

One of Remo's most popular heads is the Pinstripe, which is sort of the opposite of a dotted head. A Pinstripe has an extra ply around the circumference, which results in a very dry sound. Pinstripes are best used for batter heads on toms and bass drums. Some drummers use Pinstripe heads on snare drums, but generally you'll want a brighter sound from a snare drum than a Pinstripe head will provide.

Hydraulic

The Evans company pioneered the Hydraulic head, which is a double-ply head with a thin layer of oil between the plies, which gives an especially dry sound. Note: on regular two-ply clear heads you can often see a rainbow effect, leading some people to assume that there is oil or some other liquid between the plies; but that's just a light effect.

Imitation Calfskin

Several companies make heads that are designed to imitate the sound and feel of calfskin heads, but without the accompanying problems. (Notably, calfskin heads absorb moisture, so when it's humid, the heads expand and get flabby, but if the air suddenly dries out, the head can shrink and split.) The heads are marketed under such names as Fibreskyn (Remo) and Vintage (Aquarian). These heads have a somewhat dry sound with a mellower tone than standard plastic heads, and are preferred by some jazz drummers.

O-Ring

An O-Ring, or Zero ring, is a circular, O-shaped (or donut shaped) ring of drumhead material that can be placed over a drumhead to muffle some of the high-pitched overtones. When an O-ring is placed over a regular single-ply head, the result is similar to a Pinstripe head. An advantage of O-rings is that you can easily remove them, so that you can, in effect, switch back and forth between "regular" heads and Pinstripe-style heads in an instant. O-Rings come in different widths, so you can get more or less of the muffling effect.

TUNING

Drum tuning is sometimes a mystery, even to very accomplished drummers. The problem is, there is no standardized way of tuning drums. Guitar players, by contrast, have it easy. Each string is tuned to a specific, standardized pitch, and if your ears are not good enough to get the string in tune, electronic tuners will guide you to perfect tuning. We drummers, however, have to rely on our ears. So the first step is knowing what to listen for.

First, we need to talk just a little bit about the physics and acoustics of a drum. (Sounds scary, I know, but this is pretty simple stuff, really.) The batter head (which is the head you strike) is tuned primarily for feel. In other words, you want it to have the proper rebound. The "resonant" head (the bottom head on a snare drum or tom-tom, the front head on a bass drum) is tuned primarily for pitch.

Therefore, when replacing both heads on a drum, start with the bottom head and tune it to the pitch you want. What should that pitch be? There are no specifics here (unless you are Terry

Bozzio, who tunes his multiple tom-toms to actual pitches so that he can play melodies on his drums). So what do you listen for? Tone and resonance. Each drum has a range in which it sounds best. You need to find that area by gradually tightening the head until the drum seems to come to life, producing a clear, ringing sound.

Before you are going to get that clear tone, however, the head must be in tune with itself. That means the pitch must be the same at each opposing tuning lug (tapping at the edge of the drum, near one lug should sound the same pitch as if you tap near a lug on the opposite edge of the drum). This is where you really need to develop your ears. A drumhead produces a wide range of overtones, and it takes some practice to be able to hear the fundamental pitch.

Tuning Toms

When mounting a new bottom head, start by tightening each of the tension lugs just to the point that they are in contact with the rim. (Many drummers do this step by hand, rather than with a drum key, so there is no tension on the rim at this point.) Since the rim can wobble before all of the lugs are engaged, it is best to go back and forth when you are first installing the lugs. Imagining the drum as a clock, start with the lug at 12 o'clock, then install the lug at 6 o'clock. Then go to 1 o'clock and 7 o'clock, then 11 o'clock and 5 o'clock, and so on, working your way around the rim in a back-and-forth manner.

Once the lugs are installed evenly, begin tightening them in the same pattern. Take it slowly, no more than one full turn of the drum key at a time. As you start to feel resistance on the lugs, start turning the drum key just half a turn at a time. Keep doing this until you start to hear a tone from the head instead of a "flappy" sound. At this point, you shouldn't see any "wrinkles" in the head.

Now you need to start checking the pitch opposite each lug. If your drum has a good bearing edge that is even all the way around, and the drum is perfectly circular, the pitches should be pretty close if the tension of each lug is the same. But if there are any inconsistencies in your shell, you might need to tighten or loosen some lugs in order to get the pitches to match. One trick that many drummers use is to press lightly on the drumhead in the center with your finger. That will mute some of the overtones so that you can hear the fundamental pitch more clearly.

Once you have the head in tune with itself, continue tightening it, a quarter turn at a time, until you hear the head come alive, producing a clear, sustained tone. You often won't know exactly where that area is until you've gone past it and the drum starts to sound "choked." At that point, loosen the lugs a little bit, a quarter turn at a time, until you get back into the resonant zone.

If you are putting on a new head, you might want to leave it a little tighter at first, because it will probably stretch a bit over the first couple of days and the pitch will drop. Tuning it a little higher can also help stretch it out so that the pitch stays more consistent. But don't overdo it! If you over-tighten a head, you can stretch it to the point that it loses its resonance. (Note that when you are first tensioning a new head, you might hear some "cracking" sounds. That's just the head stretching, and it's normal.)

When you have the head where you think you want it, push down on the middle of the head with your fist. That will help stretch and settle the head. Then check the pitch at each lug again and fine tune.

To install a batter head, begin the same way. Once you get the head in tune with itself at a low pitch, gradually bring the pitch up until the drum resonates and the head has the proper tension for your playing style. Even though the top head is tensioned more for feel than for pitch, the pitches of the two heads must work together, so you need to listen for that area in which the drum sound opens up.

In many cases, the batter head will be pitched slightly lower than the resonantor head, but that's a guideline rather than a rule. If you want absolutely maximum resonance from a tom-tom, do your best to tune both heads to exactly the same pitch. If you want a deader sound from your toms, once you have the batter head in the range you want it, detune a couple of adjacent lugs (usually the ones furthest from you when the drum is in playing position) almost to the point that the head wrinkles. That will deaden the top head so that all of your resonance comes from the bottom head.

Once you have each tom-tom sounding good, you need to tune them in relation to each other. How far apart their pitches are depends on how many toms you have and your own personal taste. In any event, you want to make sure that there is enough difference between any two pitches that people can clearly hear the difference. (Otherwise, why have all those toms?)

Most drums have fuller sounds if they are tuned to the lower end of their range. A smaller drum tuned low will generally have a bigger sound than a larger drum tuned high, even if both drums are tuned to exactly the same pitch.

Tuning the Snare Drum

Snare drum tuning is very similar to tom tuning. Again, you want to start by getting each head in tune with itself, and then gradually take each head up until you get the sound and feel you want. Snare drum batter heads are generally tuned much tighter than tom batters so that you can get good bounce strokes for rolls. But don't crank a snare batter down as tight as it will go; the drum will then sound choked when you really lay into it.

Adjusting the Snares

Snares must be adjusted according to how hard you hit the drum. The most common mistake drummers make is over-tightening the snares. That might sound okay when you are tapping the drum softly, but when you lay into it, the drum will sound choked and you will lose a lot of your sound because those tight snares will prevent the bottom head from vibrating to its full potential. For a full range of sounds, snares should be at a medium tension. If you mostly play backbeats on your snare drum, and your playing range is loud, louder, and loudest, you should have your snares on the loose side so they can accept the force of the blow.

Tuning the Bass Drum

The most difficult part of getting a good bass drum sound is that you are not hearing the same thing from behind the kit as your audience is hearing from the front. So as part of the process, you need to have someone play your bass drum while you get out in front of it to hear what it really sounds like.

Generally, the only thing you want the bass drum batter head to do is move air when you hit it. It should produce a "thud," not a "boom." There are various heads that are manufactured to get this sound, or some drummers put felt strips across the batter head or rest a pillow or some other type of muffling device against the batter head inside the drum to get this effect. But choosing the right head is preferable to putting a bunch of stuff inside the drum, because that not only muffles the head, it also interferes with the resonance of the shell.

How much tone and resonance you want from your front bass drum head depends on the style of music you play, the sound you like, and the acoustic circumstances. For a while, it was customary for drummers who were playing very loud, or who were working in recording studios, not to use a front head and to stick a microphone inside the bass drum. Then, people started cutting circular holes in bass drum heads so that the resonance was deadened somewhat, but not entirely, and a microphone could be placed either inside or in front of the hole to get the maximum impact from vibration.

If you are going to be playing live without miking, don't make your bass drum too dead sounding. A lot of the ring will be soaked up by the music, but if the drum is too dry, it will not cut through the band's sound. You need a certain amount of ring for tone and projection.

If you are being miked, however, you probably want to use a front head with a hole. That will still give you a rich sound, but you'll also get a more focused impact for the mic.

ACOUSTICS

I've already mentioned this in terms of tuning the bass drum, but it applies to the drumset in general. One of the difficulties in getting a good drum sound is that drums don't sound the same close up as they do from a distance. And they don't sound the same from behind the kit as they do from in front of it. That means that when you are sitting on your drum throne, you are in the worst position to know what your drums actually sound like, because you are hearing the batter head more than the resonant head (especially when it comes to the bass drum).

Some of the "ring" you hear in your drums when you are sitting behind them is swallowed up in a large room and/or by the sound of the band. But some drummers don't realize that, so they tune their drums so that they have no ring at all. The drums sound fantastic down in these players' basements when they are playing by themselves. But when they go out on a gig with a band, the drums sound like cardboard boxes. Granted, a drum can be tuned to have so much ring that it loses its clarity, so it's not a matter of "the more ring the better," but no ring at all results in a dead-sounding drum.

CHAPTER 33
CHAPTER 33
REPAIRS

What's Ahead:
- Stripped lugs, screws, and wing nuts
- Cracked cymbals
- Cracked drumshell
- Broken drumheads
- Noisy lugs
- General maintenance
- Cleaning cymbals and drums

With all of its many parts, a drumset is prone to "breaking down" from time to time, and most drummers get pretty good at making basic repairs. Some repairs just require a screwdriver, wrench, or (everybody's favorite) duct tape. Others might require replacing a part. And some damage is so terminal that you have to replace the instrument. But even then, looking at the drumset as a whole, if you have to replace a drum, cymbal, or piece of hardware, that's only part of the total kit. Only in a catastrophic situation would you have to replace your entire drumset.

As we've already discussed in Chapter 26, you should carry various basic tools and extra parts to every gig to handle some of the most common mishaps. In this chapter, we'll look at more serious problems.

STRIPPED LUGS, SCREWS, AND WING NUTS

A lot of our stuff is tightened down with various lugs, screws, and wing nuts, and because we are continually tightening and loosening many of these items, they sometimes get stripped. That usually occurs from tightening them too much, so for starters, tighten things snugly, but don't overdo it. With many stands and holders, the use of memory collars and clamps can help hold things in place so that the wing nuts do not have to be over-tightened.

But if you do strip a lug, screw, or wing nut, obviously you need to replace it promptly. Unfortunately, in many cases it's not actually the lug, screw, or wing nut that is stripped, but rather the threaded receptacle it goes into.

If it's a drum lug, it's not too big a problem. Years ago, the lug casings themselves were threaded, and if one got stripped, you had to replace the whole thing. (That's still the case with many "tube style" lugs.) But most lug casings now have a separate receptacle that "floats" inside the casing, and replacing one of those is relatively easy and inexpensive. Of course, it means removing a drumhead so you can unbolt the lug casing from the shell, but then it's pretty easy to pop out the receptacle and replace it with a new one. Be sure you purchase a receptacle that is made for the brand and model of drum you own. They are not all the same.

If you've stripped the wing nut receptacle on a cymbal stand, snare stand, tom holder, or other piece of hardware, that might be a bigger problem. In some cases, you might be able to replace the collar of a stand. (They are sometimes held in place with a tiny hexnut-operated bolt.) But in other cases, you might have to replace an entire section of the stand, or you may even have to replace the entire stand if individual parts are not available. This is where you need to check with your local drum shop or music store. They might have pieces of broken stands that they use for parts. By the same token, if you do replace an entire stand, keep the old one for possible use as parts, the next time you strip or break a piece of a stand. (This is one reason why you might always want to buy the same brand of hardware: the parts will be interchangeable.)

CRACKED CYMBALS

You can't really "fix" the crack in a cymbal. The best you can do is "salvage" the cymbal so you can still get some use from it.

If a cymbal has a circular crack (this most often happens where the bell meets the body of the cymbal), the best you can do is try to stop the crack so that it doesn't spread all the way around the cymbal. To do that, drill a small hole at each end of the crack. Go a little bit past where you think the crack ends to be sure you get it all. Be sure to use a sharp drill bit so that you can drill the hole quickly without the bit getting too hot, or it can de-temper the cymbal metal.

If you can hear the cymbal buzzing where the crack is, you can try filing the crack between the holes you drilled so the two sides of the crack are not touching. Again, be careful about doing this in such a way that you don't get a lot of heat build-up. Do it slowly, by hand.

Do not try to fix a cracked cymbal by welding it. The heat will de-temper the metal.

If you have a crack that runs from the edge of the cymbal toward the middle, and it's not too long, the idea is to separate the sides of the crack so they don't rattle against each other. You do that by cutting a narrow, pie-shaped wedge out of the cymbal where the crack is. You should go a little bit past where you think the crack ends, because the end of the crack can be "hairline" and you won't be able to see it.

CRACKED DRUMSHELL

Once a drumshell is cracked, it has lost its "integrity" and there is not much you can do to restore it. As with cymbals, however, you might be able to salvage the drum.

A lot of it depends on just how badly the shell is cracked, and where. If it's just the outer or inner ply, you can glue it to seal the crack and prevent a rattle. A standard wood glue will work fine, but I prefer hide glue. It is essentially leather, rather than plastic, and that's what violin and guitar makers use when they are building instruments. Hide glue is porous, like the wood itself, and vibrates with the wood. Other types of glue put a layer of plastic between the wood, which doesn't vibrate as well.

If the drum is cracked to the point that it is buckled, throw it away. (But save the rims, lugs, and any other hardware; you might be able to use them for parts someday.)

BROKEN DRUMHEADS

The only reason to "fix" a drumhead, rather than replace it, is if you are in the middle of a gig and either don't have a replacement head or don't have time to change heads.

It all depends on just how badly the head is broken. If it has a small tear, you might be able to put a piece of tape over it and make it through a set, or the rest of the gig, until you can change the head. That's especially true if it is a front bass drum head or the bottom head of a tom or snare drum. Since those heads are not taking direct hits, a small piece of tape can actually do a pretty good job of retaining the head's resonance. Rather than duct tape, though, try clear packing tape. It won't have the muffling effect that you'll get from duct tape.

If the head rips all the way across the drum, don't even bother trying to tape it. Replace it as soon as possible.

NOISY LUGS

If you hear a rattling sound from your drums, it's possible that the springs inside the lug casings are rattling against the casings. You will usually notice this more on toms and bass drums. Before you start removing lugs, make sure that tom holders, spurs, floor tom legs, or other hardware isn't loose. If possible, remove any holders or other external hardware, suspend the drum with one hand and strike it with a stick (or timpani mallet). If you hear a rattle, it might be the lugs.

Before you remove the lugs, however, check to see that they are tight. If one or more of them have come loose, that's probably where your rattle is coming from. If you have tightened a lug bolt all the way and the casing is still loose, add an extra washer between the bolt and the shell. That should take care of it.

If it is indeed the springs rattling against the lug casings, there are a couple of ways to solve the problem. Some people pack the lug casings with cotton or wrap a thin piece of foam rubber around the spring. Others buy plastic surgical tubing and replace the springs with that. (You can buy a long piece of tubing and cut the pieces to fit.) Either way, that should take care of the problem.

GENERAL MAINTENANCE

Drummers who check and maintain their equipment regularly don't usually have to spend as much time and money repairing it. For starters, keep all moving parts lubricated, such as lugs, screws, wing nuts, pedals, and anything else that moves, either through playing the kit or setting it up and tearing it down.

Anytime you change drumheads, check the bolts that are holding the lugs in place to make sure they are tight. If you have one that keeps coming loose, check to see that it's not stripped. If it's not, try using a lock washer between the bolt head and the washer. Also, whenever changing heads, put a drop of oil in each lug receptacle.

Check for worn parts and replace them. Make sure that your cymbal stands have good felts under the cymbals and good sleeves around the post that goes through the hole in the cymbal. That can help prevent cracks in the cymbal around the hole. Also check pedal straps, springs, and chains. If they look like they are about to break, replace them. You don't want them breaking on a gig. (Even if they look okay, if you've had them a while, consider buying extras for backups in case one does break during a gig.)

Keep metal parts like wing nuts and screws clean and dry. Don't let them rust. That's most likely to happen with lugs and wing nuts, which another reason to keep them lubricated.

CLEANING CYMBALS AND DRUMS

Some people will tell you that you should never clean cymbals because the cleaning process will remove metal from the cymbal and ruin its sound. Others say you shouldn't clean them simply because a little dirt "mellows" out the sound. There was even a myth going around at one point that you should bury a new cymbal in the ground for a couple of weeks to "age" it.

Let's start with the last one: don't bury your cymbals. It will not do them one bit of good.

Regarding the cleaning of cymbals, however, opinions differ. A lot of it has to do with how dirty your cymbals get and how it affects the sound. Some people do, in fact, like the mellower sound that an old cymbal acquires after it gets a bit dirty. But too much dirt can muffle the sound. Also, some cymbal-cleaning methods can remove a little bit of metal. So be careful how you clean them. Most cymbal companies offer various creams and sprays for cleanig cymbals, so stick with one of those. They will be less abrasive than the general cleaners you probably have stored under the kitchen sink.

How often you clean your cymbals depends, again, on how dirty they get. If you play in places where people smoke, you will get a film over your cymbals (and drums) that should be cleaned periodically. If you use drumsticks with painted or colored tips that leave marks on your cymbals, you should clean those marks off regularly. (Better still, you should find different drumsticks.)

Sometimes you won't notice that the sound of a cymbal has changed due to dirt because it happens so gradually. But if an old cymbal is sounding dead, try cleaning it before replacing it. You just might bring it back to life.

Do not *ever* buff your cymbal with an electric buffer. That will definitely remove metal, and the heat that is generated can de-temper the metal as well, completely ruining your cymbal. When cleaning cymbals, be sure you rinse them well to get all of the cleaner off, because if you don't, that can leave a film that will muffle the cymbal and actually attract and hold more dirt.

Whereas dirt can affect the sound of a cymbal, it usually just makes drums look bad—though it can actually damage hardware in some cases by causing tarnish and rust. Drum shells can usually be cleaned with commercial furniture sprays or polishes. If you are in doubt about the effect a certain cleaner might have on your shells, test it on the bottom of the bass drum first. But if you buy the kind of polish or cleaner used on fine furniture, it should not hurt your drums.

CHAPTER 34
CHAPTER 34
CASES

What's Ahead:
- Bags
- Fiber cases
- Molded cases
- Road cases
- Moving aids

Let's get the bad pun out of the way: Drums really take a beating. (Groan!) But I'm not talking about the fact that you are constantly assailing them with sticks and mallets. They are designed to withstand that kind of beating. Granted, a head will break now and then, but that's an easy, and relatively inexpensive, fix.

Your drums are more likely to sustain serious damage while being moved than while being played, so you need to protect your instruments with cases and/or bags. A wide variety of cases and bags are available. What you need depends on your situation.

Cases generally fall into three categories: drum cases, cymbal cases, and stand/hardware cases (or "trap" cases). Let's look at the different styles.

BAGS

The term "bags" refers to soft cases that offer little protection from damage caused by sharp blows, but that will generally keep your instruments dry (and clean, if they are being stored), and make them easier to carry.

The "bags" made for drums are usually made of vinyl or nylon, and may or may not be padded. Their main advantage is that they usually have large carrying straps, many of which can serve as shoulder straps. If you tend to carry your drums yourself in a car or van, and they don't get knocked around a lot, such soft cases could be all you need, especially if you only have a few drums and they are of smaller sizes (like the ones jazz drummers use). Drum bags generally fit pretty snugly around the drum, so they don't take up extra room, and the straps can allow you to carry several drums at once by slinging a couple of them over your shoulders.

The most popular bags are for cymbals and drumsticks. You will want a well-made cymbal bag, because cymbals are heavy, but a good bag allows you to carry, say, a ride or two, a couple of crashes, a pair of hi-hats, and maybe a couple of specialty cymbals all at the same time.

Similarly, a stick bag allows you to carry quite a number of sticks, brushes, and mallets easily, and most stick bags have straps that allow them to be suspended from a floor tom so that you have easy access to your "implements" during a performance.

You can also get stand and hardware bags. Again, these allow you to pack several stands, pedals, and other hardware devices in one case for easy transporting. Most stand bags are long and narrow, so you can often just collapse the legs of cymbal and hi-hat stands for packing, without having to adjust the height. That can save you a lot of time, especially at the next set-up. Like cymbals, hardware is heavy, so you want a well-made hardware bag that can stand the weight. If you have a lot of hardware, you might even want to go with two hardware bags.

FIBER CASES

Fiber cases are probably the most popular cases for drums. They are relatively inexpensive and offer a reasonable amount of protection. It is also very easy to stack them. For added protection, some drummers line their fiber drum cases with foam rubber.

Perhaps the most popular fiber case of all is the one known as a "trap" case. It is generally a large, rectangular box that has a side compartment for cymbals, lower compartments for pedals (and possibly a snare drum), and an upper tray for stands, sticks, and other small items. I've known a lot of drummers who will have bags for their toms and bass drum, and put everything else in a fiber trap case.

As handy as trap cases can be, trying to fit every possible item into one can be tricky with today's big drumkits and double-braced hardware. Putting all of your cymbals and hardware into the same case can also result in a case that's too heavy to lift. At the very least, make sure you buy a hardware case with wheels.

Many drummers go for a fiber stand/hardware case, which is longer and narrower than a trap case, for their stands and hardware, and they put their snare drum in a separate case, and their cymbals in yet another case (or bag). It just depends on how much stuff you've got.

Fiber cymbal cases offer more protection than cymbal bags. Often they have a threaded post in the center so that you can set the bells inside each other and then secure them with a wing nut.

MOLDED CASES

Molded cases are generally of the same design as fiber cases, but are made of high-impact plastic and offer much better protection. Often, the straps are recessed so that the cases stack better.

If you do your own drum moving and are able to control how they are packed and stacked, you will probably be okay with fiber cases. But if other people are moving your drums, they might not be as careful with them, so in that situation, I would spend the extra money for molded cases. In the long run, that will be a lot less expensive than having to replace instruments that get damaged.

ROAD CASES

These are the cases made for the heaviest professional use. Road cases are generally made of wood, have metal reinforced edges and corners, and thick foam rubber linings, and can protect your drums from just about any damage.

Whereas fiber and molded drum cases are usually shaped pretty much like the drum itself, road cases are generally rectangular for easier stacking. They are made to ATA (Air Transport Association) standards, meaning that you can check them as baggage on an airline.

Many companies make custom-built ATA cases, and while you can get an individual case for each drum, cases can also be designed and built to accommodate entire drumkits. (Granted, if you have a really huge kit, you might want at least a couple of cases.) Such cases don't make sense if you are carrying your drums in your car, but if your band has a truck (and you have a roadie or two), road cases might be the way to go.

Even if you don't feel that you need road cases for your entire kit, you may want one. I know of several drummers who use an ATA case just for their snare drum. It's easy to carry, and offers the maximum protection for the most important drum in your setup.

MOVING AIDS

Large road cases are always equipped with wheels, and many fiber and molded trap cases and hardware cases are also equipped with wheels. But some are not, so you should make sure the one(s) you buy do indeed have wheels, because they will make your life a lot easier.

If you already have a large case without wheels, it's pretty easy to install them yourself. Most people cut a thick piece of plywood the same size as the bottom of the case, attach the wheels to the plywood, and then either strap or bolt the plywood onto the case. Be sure to get fairly large rubber wheels that swivel. Small wheels can get stuck easily (I can't count the times I've had to roll a case over a gravel parking lot or even over grass or dirt), and stationary wheels don't give you much flexibility.

You should also acquire a portable luggage cart. These are essentially small dollies that can be used for cases that don't have wheels. If you get one with a fairly large "platform," then you can often stack several drum cases on it and roll them all in at once.

If your drums are being piled up in a van or truck, get some bungee cords or packing straps so you can secure them against the wall of the vehicle and prevent the ones on top from falling over.

Finally, even if you have cases with wheels and/or luggage carts, from time to time you will be lifting cases. Do not lift with your lower back muscles; in other words, don't bend over, grab the case, and then straighten up. You can injure your back that way. Instead, lower yourself by bending your knees (like a deep-knee bend), grab the case, and then rise by straightening out your legs, keeping your back straight at all times.

Who's Who

What's Ahead:
- Gene Krupa
- Buddy Rich
- Max Roach
- Elvin Jones
- Tony Williams
- Ringo Starr
- Hal Blaine
- Billy Cobham
- Ginger Baker
- John Bonham
- Steve Gadd
- Neil Peart

GENE KRUPA

When Gene Krupa joined the Benny Goodman band in 1934, he became the first drumming "star" through a combination of tremendous technique and flashy showmanship. His extended solo on Goodman's hit "Sing, Sing, Sing" in 1937 led to drum solos becoming regular features of jazz concerts. After leaving Goodman, Krupa led his own very successful big band and then toured with Jazz at the Philharmonic for many years. In 1954, he and drummer Cozy Cole started a drum school in New York City, and Krupa spent the next 20 years teaching and playing with small groups around New York. He died in 1973.

Photo Courtesy of Slingerland Drum Company

Krupa combined the styles of such early jazz drumming greats as Baby Dodds, Zutty Singleton, and Chick Webb. With a formidable technique grounded in the drum rudiments, he created an original style that paved the way for such later big band drummers as Buddy Rich and Louie Bellson. He also influenced many young rock drummers, and Peter Criss said that his extended solo with Kiss was based on Krupa's "Drum Boogie."

Essential Tunes

"Sing, Sing, Sing"	Benny Goodman	*The Best of Benny Goodman*
"Drum Boogie"	Gene Krupa	*Hot Drums*
"Drummin' Man"	Gene Krupa	*Drummin' Man*

BUDDY RICH

Buddy Rich used to call himself "the world's greatest drummer," and a lot of people agreed. Considered by many to be the most technically accomplished drummer who ever lived, Rich began his career at age three in vaudeville, billed as "Traps the Drum Wonder." As vaudeville faded when Rich was in his late teens, he began working with jazz groups and soon made a name for himself in bands led by Artie Shaw (featuring a young singer named Frank Sinatra), Tommy Dorsey, and Harry James. Rich led several small groups and big bands of his own, the most well-known being the big band he led from 1966 until his death in 1987. Rich was best known for his fiery solos, which featured blazing single-stroke snare drum rolls.

Photo by Rick Mattingly

Essential Tunes

"West Side Story Medley"	Buddy Rich Big Band	*Swingin' New Big Band*
"Love For Sale"	Buddy Rich Big Band	*Big Swing Face*
"Channel 1 Suite"	Buddy Rich Big Band	*Mercy Mercy*

MAX ROACH

As the Big Band era of the 1930s and early '40s gave way to the Bebop era of the late 1940s and '50s, Max Roach became the most important bop drummer through his work with bebop founders Charlie "Bird" Parker (saxophone) and Dizzy Gillespie (trumpet). Roach was at the forefront of a new drumming style in which the ride cymbal was the most important element of the drumkit, and his ability to play extremely fast ride patterns set a new standard for drumming excellence. Roach co-led an influential group with trumpeter Clifford Brown for several years, and then led several groups of his own after Brown's untimely death.

Photo courtesy of Photofest, Inc.

Roach also pioneered solo drum compositions, such as "The Drum Also Waltzes," and he organized the first jazz percussion ensemble, M'Boom. Roach brought a new complexity and sophistication to jazz drumming, and he also used his music to address political concerns such as racism.

Essential Tunes

"The Drum Also Waltzes"	Max Roach	*Drums Unlimited*
"I'll Remember April"	Clifford Brown and Max Roach	*At Basin Street*
"Un Poco Loco"	Bud Powell	*The Amazing Bud Powell, Vol. 1*
"Salt Peanuts"	Dizzy Gillespie and Charlie Parker	*Jazz at Massey Hall*
"Prayer/Protest/Peace"	Max Roach	*We Insist! Freedom Now Suite*

ELVIN JONES

His pioneering work with saxophonist John Coltrane made Elvin Jones the most important jazz drummer of the 1960s, and one of the most influential jazz drummers of all time. Using all of the elements of his drumkit as a single instrument, Jones propelled the time forward with a "rolling and tumbling" approach that featured multiple layers of rhythm exploding from his drums and cymbals. Elvin's drumming often sounded ferocious, but he could also play with extreme delicacy, and his brush playing could evoke the hissing of a snake. After leaving Coltrane, Jones led his own groups until his death in 2004. Many rock drummers, including Santana's Michael Shrieve and the Doors' John Densmore, regard Elvin as a major influence on their styles.

Photo by Rick Mattingly

Essential Tunes

"Acknowledgement"	John Coltrane	*A Love Supreme*
"Ascension"	John Coltrane	*Ascension*
"Keiko's Birthday March"	Elvin Jones	*Puttin' It All Together*
"Summertime"	Elvin Jones and Richard Davis	*Heavy Sounds*
"Three Card Molly"	Elvin Jones	*Genesis*

TONY WILLIAMS

First coming to national prominence at age 17 when he joined the Miles Davis Quintet (along with saxophonist Wayne Shorter, pianist Herbie Hancock, and bassist Ron Carter), Tony Williams helped define the "fusion" drumming style of the late 1960s by blending elements of rock drumming with his mastery of swing and bop. Among his stylistic characteristics were the freeing up of the hi-hat from its traditional role of maintaining beats 2 and 4, and a more pulse-oriented approach to the ride cymbal, which foreshadowed the use of straight-eighth rock rhythms in jazz. After leaving Davis, Williams explored rock and funk rhythms in a series of solo albums while continuing to play jazz with such groups as VSOP and The Great Jazz Trio. During the 1980s, Williams released several jazz-oriented solo albums that featured his own compositions. Williams suffered a fatal heart attack in 1997 at age 51.

Photo by Rick Mattingly

Essential Tunes

"Maiden Voyage"	Herbie Hancock	*Maiden Voyage*
"Freedom Jazz Dance"	Miles Davis	*Miles Smiles*
"Nefertiti	Miles Davis	*Nefertiti*
"Emergency"	Tony Williams' Lifetime	*Emergency*
"Snake Oil"	Tony Williams	*Believe It*

RINGO STARR

In the 1960s, seeing Ringo Starr with the Beatles inspired countless young boys to become drummers. His style was simple and basic, to the point that some people dismissed him as being the least talented member of the group, and merely an adequate drummer. But Ringo had a great time feel, and the parts he created for the songs written by Lennon/McCartney and George Harrison were very creative and served the music perfectly.

Photo courtesy of Photofest, Inc.

Essential Tunes

"Ticket to Ride"	The Beatles	*Help*
"Rain"	The Beatles	*Hey Jude*
"In My Life"	The Beatles	*Rubber Soul*
"Come Together"	The Beatles	*Abbey Road*
"Carry That Weight"	The Beatles	*Abbey Road*
"Tomorrow Never Knows"	The Beatles	*Revolver*

HAL BLAINE

During the 1960s and early '70s, Hal Blaine was one of the busiest studio drummers on the West Coast, and although his name seldom appeared on album credits, his drumming was heard on numerous hits by such artists as Elvis Presley, the Crystals, the Ronettes, Sam Cooke, the Byrds, the Beach Boys, Jan and Dean, The Mamas & The Papas, the Monkees, Frank Sinatra, Herb Alpert & the Tijuana Brass, Johnny Rivers, Gary Lewis & the Playboys, the Association, Paul Revere & the Raiders, Simon & Garfunkel, the Carpenters, and countless others, including many records produced by the legendary Phil Spector. He played on 40 number-one records and eight of the records he played on won GRAMMY® Awards for Record of the Year. He was inducted into the Rock and Roll Hall of Fame in 2000.

Essential Tunes

"Return to Sender"	Elvis Presley	*Elvis' Gold Records*
"Be My Baby"	The Ronettes	*Best of the Ronettes*
"A Taste of Honey"	Herb Alpert & the Tijuana Brass	*Whipped Cream and Other Delights*
"Good Vibrations"	The Beach Boys	*Smiley Smile*
"Aquarius/Let the Sun Shine"	Fifth Dimension	*Age of Aquarius*

BILLY COBHAM

Through his work with the Mahavishnu Orchestra and a series of influential solo albums, Billy Cobham became the biggest drumming star of the 1970s, appealing to jazz drummers as well as rock drummers. Using a large drumkit with double bass drums, Cobham mixed the power of rock with the sophistication of jazz and a remarkable technical command that included mastery of the odd-time signatures used in Mahavishnu tunes. Recordings with a variety of other

Photo by David Redfern/Redferns Music Picture Library

artists proved Cobham to be adept at straight-ahead jazz and funk as well, but many best remember Cobham's drumming of the '70s for his blazing single-stroke rolls around his large kit.

Essential Tunes

"Right Off"	Miles Davis	*A Tribute to Jack Johnson*
"One Word"	Mahavishnu Orchestra	*Birds of Fire*
"Quadrant 4"	Billy Cobham	*Spectrum*

GINGER BAKER

Playing with Cream in the 1960s, Ginger Baker became the first rock drumming superstar, and was held in equal esteem to his band mates, guitarist Eric Clapton and bassist Jack Bruce. Performing on a large double bass kit, Baker mixed African rhythms with blues, rock, and jazz grooves. Whereas most rock drummers kept time on the hi-hat or ride cymbal, and just used the bass drum and snare drum for basic beats and backbeats, Baker often used his tom-toms and bass drums as the main timekeeping elements, creating a thunderous style of drumming that propelled Cream's music forward and filled out the sound of the first "power trio." After Cream broke up, Baker played in Blind Faith and then started his own group, Ginger Baker's Airforce, which included African musicians. Baker remains active, and in recent years has recorded with jazz guitarist Bill Frisell.

Photo by Ian Dickson/Redferns Music Picture Library

Essential Tunes

"Sunshine of Your Love"	Cream	*Disraeli Gears*
"White Room"	Cream	*Wheels of Fire*
"Toad"	Cream	*Wheels of Fire*

JOHN BONHAM

As the drummer for Led Zeppelin in the 1970s, John Henry "Bonzo" Bonham became the definitive hard rock/metal drummer, influencing scores of drummers who came after him. He played with tremendous power and passion, but also possessed a sense of swing and a finesse that gave Zeppelin's music a great deal of forward momentum. During solos, he would often play with his bare hands, adding a very soulful quality to his rhythmic adventures. Bonham died tragically at age 33 on September 25, 1980, and Led Zeppelin subsequently disbanded, as the other members felt that no one could replace him. Since Bonzo's death, his son, Jason Bonham, has also made a name for himself as a drummer, including performances with the surviving members of Led Zeppelin when the group was inducted into the Rock and Roll Hall of Fame in 1994.

Photo by David Redfern/Redferns Music Picture Library

Essential Tunes

"Moby Dick"	Led Zeppelin	*The Song Remains the Same*
"Immigrant Song"	Led Zeppelin	*Led Zeppelin III*

"The Ocean"	Led Zeppelin	*Houses of the Holy*
"Rock and Roll"	Led Zeppelin	*Led Zeppelin IV*
"Kashmir"	Led Zeppelin	*Physical Graffiti*

STEVE GADD

Steve Gadd first came to prominence as a jazz drummer, but soon became known for his ability to play a wide variety of styles, and he is especially revered for his funk drumming. During the 1970s and '80s, Gadd was one of the busiest studio drummers in New York, playing on records by such artists as Paul Simon, George Benson, Jim Hall, Rickie Lee Jones, Paul McCartney, Carly Simon, Jim Croce, Manhattan Transfer, Stuff, Steps, and David Sanborn. But unlike most studio musicians whose names were unknown by most music fans, Gadd established a strong identity through his work with such artists as Chick Corea, Steely Dan, and his own group, the Gadd Gang. In the mid-1990s Gadd began touring and recording frequently with Eric Clapton, and also has toured with James Taylor, Paul Simon, and Al Jarreau.

Photo by Rick Mattingly

Essential Tunes

"50 Ways to Leave Your Lover"	Paul Simon	*Still Crazy After All These Years*
"Late in the Evening"	Paul Simon	*One Trick Pony*
"Aja"	Steely Dan	*Aja*
"Samba Song"	Chick Corea	*Friends*
"Quartet No. 2, Part 2"	Chick Corea	*Three Quartets*
"Sunshine of Your Love"	Eric Clapton	*One More Car, One More Rider*

NEIL PEART

During the 1980s, and continuing to this day, Neil Peart has earned the respect of countless drummers who consider him a true drum god for his intricate prog-rock drum grooves and superbly constructed drum solos, all played with finesse and power on a gargantuan drumset. Peart not only raised the bar on drum technique, but he also became a role model for many through his writings (lyrics, books, and magazine articles) and his work ethic. Like all the drummers discussed in this chapter, Peart has proven that a good drummer is just as much a *musician* as anyone else in the band.

Photo by Fin Costello/Redferns Music Picture Library

Essential Tunes

"Tom Sawyer"	Rush	*Moving Pictures*
"YYZ"	Rush	*Exit Stage Left*
"Freewill"	Rush	*Permanent Waves*
"Natural Science"	Rush	*Permanent Waves*
"Mystic Rhythms"	Rush	*Power Windows*

APPENDIX

REFERENCE SHEET

DRUMSET ARRANGEMENT

Pictured below are front and overhead views of the most standard arrangement of a 5-piece drumset with cymbals.

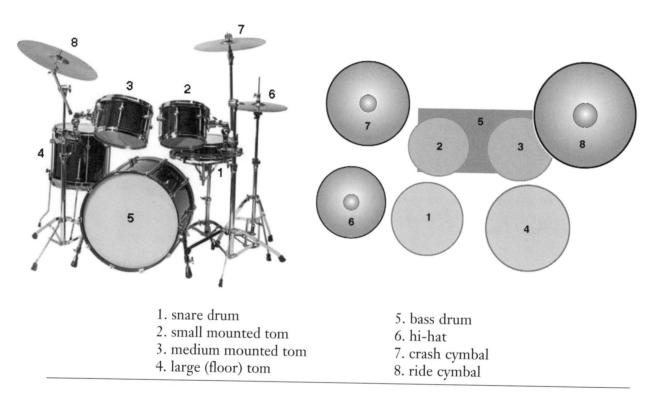

1. snare drum	5. bass drum
2. small mounted tom	6. hi-hat
3. medium mounted tom	7. crash cymbal
4. large (floor) tom	8. ride cymbal

DRUMSET NOTATION KEY

Here is the most typical arrangement of drumset instruments on a staff, based on the Percussive Arts Society Guidelines to Standardized Drumset Notation.

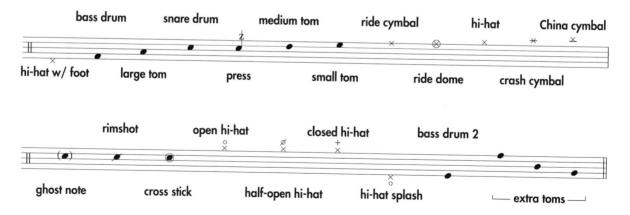

RHYTHM NOTATION CHART

Notes indicate the *pitch* and *duration* of a musical tone (how long it lasts within a measure). There are different kinds of notes to indicate different durations:

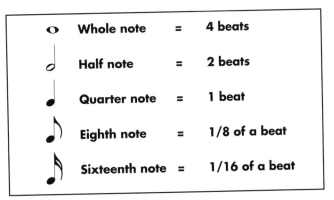

𝅝	**Whole note**	=	**4 beats**
𝅗𝅥	**Half note**	=	**2 beats**
𝅘𝅥	**Quarter note**	=	**1 beat**
𝅘𝅥𝅮	**Eighth note**	=	**1/8 of a beat**
𝅘𝅥𝅯	**Sixteenth note**	=	**1/16 of a beat**

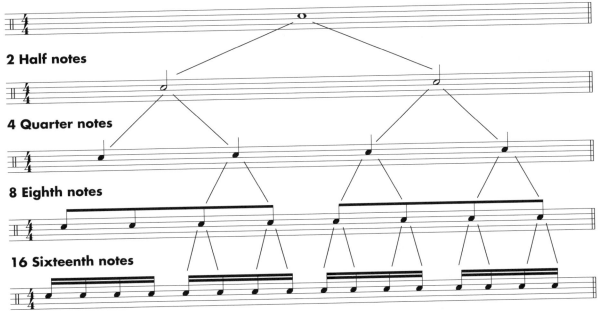

1 Whole note

2 Half notes

4 Quarter notes

8 Eighth notes

16 Sixteenth notes

RESTS

Rests indicate moments of silence. The most common rests correspond to the notes above.

Whole rest

Half rest

Quarter rest

Eighth rest

Sixteenth rest

WHO'S WHO BIG LIST

Alex Acuña
Styles: jazz, Latin
Played with: Weather Report

Steven Adler
Style: rock
Played with: Guns N' Roses

Tommy Aldridge
Style: rock
Played with: Black Oak Arkansas, Ozzy Osbourne, Whitesnake, Pat Travers

Rick Allen
Style: rock
Played with: Def Leppard

Jerry Allison
Styles: rock, rockabilly, country
Played with: Buddy Holly, Waylon Jennings

Carmine Appice
Style: rock
Played with: Vanilla Fudge, Cactus, Beck, Bogert & Appice, Rod Stewart

Kenny Aronoff
Styles: rock, studio
Played with: John Mellencamp, Melissa Etheridge, Bob Seeger, Smashing Pumpkins, John Fogerty

Ginger Baker
Styles: rock, blues
Played with: Cream, Blind Faith, Airforce

Eddie Bayers
Styles: country, studio
Played with: George Strait, Ricky Skaggs, Wynona, Toby Keith, Kenny Chesney, Hank Williams Jr., Reba McEntire

Frank Beard
Style: rock
Played with: ZZ Top

Carter Beauford
Style: rock
Played with: Dave Matthews Band

Louis Bellson
Style: jazz
Played with: Duke Ellington, Tommy Dorsey, Oscar Peterson

Benny Benjamin
Styles: funk, soul
Played with: Wide variety of Motown artists, including Supremes, Temptations, Smokey Robinson

Gregg Bissonette
Styles: rock, jazz, fusion
Played with: David Lee Roth, Maynard Ferguson, Ringo Starr

Hal Blaine
Styles: rock, studio
Played with: The Beach Boys, Frank Sinatra, The Mamas & The Papas, Phil Spector

Art Blakey
Style: jazz
Played with: Thelonious Monk, Art Blakey's Jazz Messengers

John Bonham
Style: rock
Played with: Led Zeppelin

Terry Bozzio
Styles: rock, fusion
Played with: Frank Zappa, Missing Persons, Jeff Beck, UK, Brecker Bros.

Don Brewer
Style: rock
Played with: Grank Funk Railroad

Bill Bruford
Styles: rock, jazz, fusion
Played with: Yes, Earthworks, King Crimson, UK

Clem Burke
Style: rock
Played with: Blondie

Jimmy Chamberlin
Style: rock
Played with: Smashing Pumpkins

Dennis Chambers
Styles: rock, funk, jazz, fusion
Played with: Parliament/Funkadelic, Santana, John Scofield, Steely Dan

Gary Chester
Styles: rock, jazz, studio
Played with: Isley Brothers, Burt Bacharach, Jim Croce, Drifters, Laura Nyro, Neil Sedaka, Aretha Franklin

Kenny Clarke
Style: jazz
Played with: Dizzy Gillespie, Modern Jazz Quartet, Miles Davis, Clarke-Boland Big Band

Jimmy Cobb
Style: jazz
Played with: Miles Davis, Wynton Kelly, Wes Montgomery

Billy Cobham
Styles: jazz, fusion
Played with: Mahavishnu Orchestra, Dreams

Vinnie Colaiuta
Styles: rock, jazz, fusion, studio
Played with: Frank Zappa, Sting, Joni Mitchell, Chick Corea

Phil Collins
Style: rock
Played with: Genesis

Bobby Colomby
Styles: rock, jazz, fusion
Played with: Blood, Sweat & Tears

Tré Cool
Style: rock
Played with: Green Day

Stewart Copeland
Style: rock
Played with: The Police

Dino Danelli
Style: Rock
Played with: Young Rascals

Sly Dunbar
Style: reggae
Played with: Peter Tosh, Black Uhuru, Mighty Diamonds

Jack DeJohnette
Style: jazz
Played with: Miles Davis, Keith Jarrett, New Directions, Charles Lloyd, Special Edition

Sheila E
Styles: rock, Latin
Played with: Prince, George Duke, Herbie Hancock, Billy Cobham, Marvin Gaye

Peter Erskine
Styles: jazz, rock, fusion
Played with: Weather Report, Maynard Ferguson, Steps Ahead, Joni Mitchell, Steely Dan

Anton Fig
Styles: rock, studio
Played with: Bob Dylan, Paul Shaffer Band (David Letterman show), Ace Frehley, Mick Jagger, Kiss, Cyndi Lauper

Mick Fleetwood
Style: rock
Played with: Fleetwood Mac

Steve Gadd
Styles: rock, jazz, funk, studio
Played with: Chick Corea, Eric Clapton, James Taylor, Steely Dan, Paul Simon

David Garibaldi
Style: funk
Played with: Tower of Power

Dave Grohl
Style: rock
Played with: Nirvana, Foo Fighters

Roger Hawkins
Styles: soul, studio
Played with: Eric Clapton, Aretha Franklin, Paul Simon, Wilson Pickett, Traffic

Roy Haynes
Style: jazz
Played with: Charlie Parker, Gary Burton, Chick Corea, Thelonious Monk, Bud Powell, John Coltrane

Levon Helm
Style: rock
Played with: The Band, Bob Dylan

Horacio "El Negro" Hernandez
Styles: Latin, jazz
Played with: Michel Camilo, Roy Hargrove,
Paquito D'Rivera, Santana

Al Jackson
Styles: rock, funk
Played with: Booker T. & the MG's,
Otis Redding, Sam & Dave

Elvin Jones
Style: jazz
Played with: John Coltrane, Sonny Rollins,
Elvin Jones Jazz Machine, Great Jazz
Trio, McCoy Tyner, Grant Green

Kenney Jones
Style: rock
Played with: Faces, The Who

"Papa" Jo Jones
Style: jazz
Played with: Count Basie

Philly Joe Jones
Style: jazz
Played with: Miles Davis, Bill Evans, Tadd
Dameron

Steve Jordan
Styles: rock, funk, jazz, fusion
Played with: Keith Richards, John Mayer,
Blues Brothers

Jim Keltner
Styles: rock, jazz, studio
Played with: John Lennon, George
Harrison, Boz Scaggs, Little Village,
Leon Russell, Gary Lewis, Traveling
Wilburys, Bob Dylan

Simon Kirke
Style: rock
Played with: Bad Company

Joey Kramer
Style: rock
Played with: Aerosmith

Gene Krupa
Style: jazz
Played with: Benny Goodman

Russ Kunkel
Styles: rock, studio
Played with: James Taylor, Linda Ronstadt,
Art Garfunkel, David Crosby

Tommy Lee
Style: rock
Played with: Mötley Crüe

Harvey Mason
Styles: jazz, funk, studio
Played with: George Benson, Herbie
Hancock, Grover Washington Jr., Bob
James

Nick Mason
Style: rock
Played with: Pink Floyd

Nicko McBrain
Style: heavy metal
Played with: Iron Maiden

Chet McKracken
Style: rock
Played with: Doobie Brothers

Mitch Mitchell
Style: rock
Played with: Jimi Hendrix

Joseph "Zigaboo" Modeliste
Style: funk
Played with: The Meters

Stanton Moore
Style: funk
Played with: Galactic

Airto Moreira
Styles: jazz, Brazilian
Played with: Miles Davis, Chick Corea,
Weather Report, Flora Purim

Joe Morello
Style: jazz
Played with: Dave Brubeck, Marion
McPartland

Rod Morgenstein
Styles: rock, fusion
Played with: Dixie Dregs, Winger, Jazz Is
Dead, Steve Morse Band

Keith Moon
Style: rock
Played with: The Who

Larry Mullen, Jr.
Style: rock
Played with: U2

Andy Newmark
Styles: rock, funk
Played with: Sly & the Family Stone, Carly
    Simon, John Lennon, Roxy Music

Carl Palmer
Style: rock
Played with: Emerson, Lake & Palmer, Asia

Earl Palmer
Styles: rock, studio
Played with: Little Richard, Fats Domino,
    Lloyd Price, Smiley Lewis

Neil Peart
Style: rock
Played with: Rush

Doane Perry
Style: rock
Played with: Jethro Tull

Simon Phillips
Style: rock
Played with: Jeff Beck, Pete Townshend, Toto

Jeff Porcaro
Styles: rock, studio
Played with: Toto, Steely Dan

Mike Portnoy
Style: rock
Played with: Dream Theater, Neal Morse,
    Transatlantic

Bernard Purdie
Styles: rock, funk, jazz, studio
Played with: Aretha Franklin, King Curtis,
    James Brown, B.B. King

Buddy Rich
Style: jazz
Played with: Artie Shaw, Tommy Dorsey,
    Harry James, Buddy Rich Band

Max Roach
Style: jazz

Played with: Charlie Parker, Bud Powell,
    Dizzy Gillespie, Clifford Brown,
    M'Boom

Gina Schock
Style: rock
Played with: Go-Go's

Danny Seraphine
Styles: rock, jazz
Played with: Chicago

Michael Shrieve
Styles: rock, jazz
Played with: Santana

Chad Smith
Style: rock
Played with: Red Hot Chili Peppers

Steve Smith
Styles: rock, jazz, fusion
Played with: Journey, Vital Information

Matt Sorum
Style: rock
Played with: Guns N' Roses, Velvet Revolver

John "Jabo" Starks
Styles: funk, soul
Played with: James Brown

Ringo Starr
Style: rock
Played with: The Beatles

Clyde Stubblefield
Styles: funk, soul
Played with: James Brown

Roger Taylor
Style: rock
Played with: Queen

Tico Torres
Style: rock
Played with: Bon Jovi

Alex Van Halen
Style: rock
Played with: Van Halen

Lars Ulrich
Style: rock
Played with: Metallica

Chad Wackerman
Styles: rock, jazz
Played with: Frank Zappa, Allan
    Holdsworth, Steve Vai, Andy Summers

Charlie Watts
Styles: rock, jazz
Played with: Rolling Stones, Charlie
    Watts Orchestra

Dave Weckl
Style: jazz
Played with: Chick Corea, Michel
    Camilo, Anthony Jackson, Mike
    Stern

Alan White
Style: rock
Played with: Yes, Plastic Ono Band

Lenny White
Style: jazz
Played with: Chick Corea's Return to
    Forever, Miles Davis, Freddy
    Hubbard, Azteca, Stanley Clarke

Max Weinberg
Styles: rock, jazz
Played with: Bruce Springsteen

Tony Williams
Style: jazz
Played with: Miles Davis, Lifetime,
    Herbie Hancock, Eric Dolphy, Stan
    Getz, VSOP

Zoro
Styles: funk, rock
Played with: Lenny Kravitz, Bobby
    Brown, New Edition

CD TRACK LISTING

1 whole, half, and quarter patterns
2 quarter and eighth patterns
3 quarter, eighth and sixteenth patterns
4 basic beat
5 quarter feel
6 eighth feel
7 swing feel
8 sixteenth feel
9 quarter-feel rock groove
10 eighth-feel rock groove
11 quarter-feel groove
12 sixteenth-feel groove
13 alternating sixteenth groove
14 shuffle groove
15 sixteenth fill
16 triplet fill
17 groove with fill
18 fill variations
19 jazz feel with brushes
20 jazz ballad feel with brushes
21 ghost notes
22 mixed meters: constant note values
23 mixed meters: constant pulse
24 two against three
25 three against four
26 double bass eighths
27 double bass sixteenths
28 double bass triplets
29 double bass shuffle
30 Latin instruments
31 rock shuffle
32 rock shuffle variation
33 Bo Diddley beat
34 Bo Diddley variation
35 blues shuffle
36 blues shuffle variation
37 12/8 blues
38 12/8 blues variation
39 half-time shuffle
40 jazz time 1
41 jazz time 2
42 jazz time 3
43 jazz time on hi-hat
44 snare drum independence
45 snare and bass independence
46 anticipated beat
47 breaking up time
48 double-time jazz
49 half-time jazz
50 jazz waltz
51 5/4 jazz
52 7/4 jazz
53 jazz-rock
54 cha-cha-cha
55 rumba
56 songo
57 nanigo
58 mozambique
59 samba
60 samba variation
61 bossa nova
62 batucada
63 beguine
64 tango
65 bolero
66 reggae
67 heavy rock groove
68 heavy rock variation
69 eighth groove with quarter ride
70 shuffle rock
71 sixteenth groove with quarter ride
72 eighth rock groove
73 sixteenth groove
74 progressive rock in 9/8
75 progressive rock in 5/4
76 progressive rock in 10/8
77 progressive rock in 4/4
78 progressive rock in 3/4
79 progressive rock in 7/8
80 basic funk
81 funk with open hi-hat
82 sixteenth funk
83 offbeat funk
84 offbeat funk variation
85 linear funk
86 linear funk variation
87 special cymbals
88 snare drum roll
89 roll variation
90 roll variation
91 "Walk This Way"
92 "No Reply at All"
93 "Smoke on the Water"
94 "Cissy Strut"
95 "Nice to Know You"

ABOUT THE AUTHOR

Rick Mattingly has written articles on drummers and drumming for *Modern Drummer*, *Percussive Notes*, *Drum*, *Jazziz*, and *Down Beat* magazines, as well as *The New Grove Dictionary of Jazz*. He is the author of *The Drummer's Time* (a collection of interviews with great jazz drummers) and of the instructional books *Creative Timekeeping* and *The Hal Leonard Snare Drum Method*, and co-author of *The Drumset Musician* (with Rod Morgenstein) and *Fast Track Drums* Books 1 and 2 (with Blake Neely). He has also edited instructional books by drummers Peter Erskine, Joe Morello, Gary Chester, Rod Morgenstein, Bill Bruford, Carl Palmer, Bob Moses, Casey Scheuerell, and others. He was an editor at *Modern Drummer* magazine for nine years and has been Publications Editor of the Percussive Arts Society since 1994. He holds a Bachelor's Degree in Music Education and a Master's Degree in Percussion Performance, and has played in symphony orchestras as well as rock and jazz bands. He runs an innovative percussion program at St. Xavier High School in Louisville, Kentucky.